Developments in Geography Teaching

The Changing Classroom

General Editor: John Eggleston

Developments in Art Teaching
Terence Wooff

Developments in Design Education
John Eggleston

Developments in Drama Teaching
Lynn McGregor

Developments in Early Childhood Education
Janet Lancaster and Joan Gaunt

Developments in English Teaching
Michael Saunders

Developments in Geography Teaching
Philip Boden

Developments in History Teaching
Ian Steele

Developments in Mathematics Teaching
F. R. Watson

Developments in Modern Language Teaching
Colin Wringe

Developments in Social Studies Teaching
Denis Gleeson and Geoff Whitty

Developments in Geography Teaching

Philip Boden

Open Books
London

First published in 1976 by Open Books Publishing Ltd,
87–89 Shaftesbury Avenue, LONDON W1V 7AD

© Philip Boden 1976

Hardback: ISBN 0 7291 0038 3

Paperback: ISBN 0 7291 0033 2

This title is available in both hardback and paperback editions. The paperback edition is sold subject to the condition that it shall not, by way of trade or otherwise, be lent, re-sold, hired out or otherwise circulated in any form of binding or cover other than that in which it is published and without a similar condition, including this condition, being imposed on the subsequent purchaser.

All rights reserved. No part of the publication may be reproduced or transmitted in any form or by any means, electronic or mechanical, including photocopy, recording, or any information storage and retrieval system, without permission in writing from the publisher.

Text set in 11/12pt Photon Imprint, printed by photolithography, and bound in Great Britain at The Pitman Press, Bath

To my parents

Acknowledgements

My primary thanks must go to all those with whom I have had the privilege to learn. My own teachers, while I was a pupil at school and a student at university, inspired my interest in geography. My fellow geography teachers and pupils at the schools in which I have taught encouraged in me an understanding of how geography might be taught. My colleagues and students at Keele have given me a wider perspective on geography in education, and the opportunity to continue to learn.

I am grateful to my fellow geographers, Gordon Elliott, Margaret Saunders, Alan Wheatley, Tony Gelsthorpe, Ken Briggs and David Jones, who have described the varied nature of innovation in action, in the chapters of Part II of the book.

The author of chapter 8 and the publishers would like to thank the following for permission to reproduce material used in the chapter: the Schools Council for the material from G. Hickman, J. Reynolds and H. Tolley, *A New Professionalism for a Changing Geography* (1973), and the University of Cambridge Local Examinations Syndicate for diagrams from the *Examination Regulations on the G.C.E. O Level, Schools Council 14–18 Geography Project* (Subject Number 268).

Finally, my immediate personal thanks go to all my colleagues, family and friends for bearing with me while I have been writing this book, and to Mrs Sherril Bell for typing the manuscript.

January 1976 *Philip Boden*
Keele

Contents

Acknowledgements	vi
Editor's introduction	ix
Introduction	xi

Part I Present practice and prescription

1	What is school geography?	1
2	How is geography learnt?	21
3	Where does geography stand in the curriculum?	37
4	When is geography learnt?	46
5	Why learn geography?	53

Part II Innovation in action

6	Project and school working together *Gordon Elliott and Margaret Saunders*	59
7	Implementing a resource based project *Alan Wheatley*	70
8	Beyond the curriculum package *Tony Gelsthorpe*	80

9	A new examination syllabus *Ken Briggs*	91
10	A school based development *David Jones*	100

Part III Future change

11	The knowledge explosion	107
12	Handling the data	111
13	Environmental impact studies	115
14	Community, home and school	119
15	Geography for the future	122
	References *and* Name index	123
	Subject index	126

Editor's introduction

The theme of this series of books is the changing classroom. Everyone knows that schools change – that despite all the influences of tradition things aren't the same as they used to be. Yet during the past decade the change has been on such an unprecedented scale that in many ways schools have become surprising places not only to those who work with them – like parents and employers – but even to those who work in them, like teachers and students.

There are many reasons for these changes. Some are organisational, like the move to comprehensive secondary schooling, the raising of the school leaving age, new pre-school classes, and 'destreaming', where children of all abilities work together. But even more spring from the way the teacher works in the classroom – from the increasing emphasis on individual methods, on creativity rather than remembering, on new patterns of assessment and examination, and on the use of a wide variety of project methods.

Such changes have certainly transformed the life of many classrooms and made school a different place for teachers and their students. This series is about life in those classrooms, for it is here that we can not only see change but understand it and get to grips with its effects on young people and on the society in which they will live.

In this volume Philip Boden writes about new developments in the teaching of geography. For many years geography has held not only an established place but also an unchanging one in the curriculum.

But in the past decade there have been dramatic changes. The old emphasis on description has been replaced in many schools by an emphasis on development. New systematic studies that focus upon location have tended to supersede the previously dominant regional studies. Quantified approaches have been developed in areas where, until recently, they scarcely existed. Why have these changes taken place? Can they equip children more fully to solve the problems of the resources and ecology of our society? How are they reflected in classroom practice? With the aid of case studies of the new approaches Philip Boden, an experienced geography teacher, analyses the new situation and reviews the prospects for the new curriculum in geography.

John Eggleston

Introduction

There has been much discussion about changes in geography teaching in recent years. Most discussion relates to the developments that have been taking place in universities during the last fifteen years. It favours considered adoption of the latest approaches and techniques in schools. This introductory book attempts to show how the important developments fit into the context of present day school geography as a whole, to illustrate specific changes and to ask questions about the nature of possible future trends. It does this by raising five basic questions.

The first of these questions is: *What is school geography?* To help us towards an answer, present practice will be reviewed along with the advice offered to teachers as to what it ought to be. The second question is: *How is geography learnt?* Methods of data collection, presentation and analysis will be considered in the context of approaches to the learning of skills, knowledge and attitudes. The third is: *Where does geography stand in the curriculum?* Links and associations with other subjects will be considered here. The fourth question is: *When is geography learnt?* The pattern and sequence of syllabuses will be reviewed and what is thought to be appropriate for particular age and ability levels discussed. Lastly: *Why learn geography?* Taking into account the answers to the previous questions, possible immediate and longer-term aims in learning geography will be examined.

By considering the questions separately in turn, it is hoped that it will be possible to offer a coherent view of the diversity and complexity of contemporary school geography. The evidence available from classrooms, published resources, and examination syllabuses and papers allows a range of styles and significant trends to be identified.

PART I
Present practice and prescription

1 What is school geography?

Most geography lessons have a common purpose which reflect the literal meaning of the word geography. They describe and attempt to explain the locational nature of features at or near the Earth's surface.

Characteristic of recent definitions is the statement, 'the questions about location, spatial structure and spatial process which we ask and answer, distinguish geography from the other sciences' (Abler, Adams and Gould 1970). This, like most definitions, emphasises the one key interest of geography which gives it coherence and continuity as a study — namely, concern with understanding how features come to be located where they are in terrestrial space.

School geography uses a number of organising frameworks to describe where things are and to explain how they are locationally related.

The frameworks

Three basic frameworks are currently used. They can be described as *conceptual*, *systematic* and *regional*. Brief definitions to distinguish the three will be useful before noting the background to their use in geography and then looking at them separately. This is especially so because the term 'conceptual', which brings together in one approach many recent developments, may be less familiar than the other two. Therefore it is in particular need of clarification.

In *conceptual* studies focus is on ideas. That is, emphasis is placed on the significant terms and theories which geographers use to describe and explain the characteristic of location. Many simple terms are used to make vital distinctions about location and these need to be understood clearly. For example, it is important to distinguish use of the terms 'site' and 'situation'. Site is used to define the actual absolute location occupied by a feature. Situation is used to define the location of a site relative to the site of other features. Focus can also be on more complex ideas, such as those found within theories. There is, for example, a group of theories related to the degree of accessibility of locations. The prime purpose of geography lessons organised conceptually is to enable pupils to learn ideas about location which can be applied generally.

In *systematic* studies focus is on distinctive features in the landscape and their particular locational characteristics. It is not on general ideas which can be applied to all possible features. For example, study may be made of a class of features, like villages, towns and cities and their distinctive locational characteristics alone. Similarly, but quite separately, study may be made of patterns of agricultural land use or glaciated landscapes. The aim is for pupils to learn about the specified locational characteristics of named features.

In *regional* studies presentation is organised around subunits of the Earth's surface, not general ideas or particular features. Study is made of areas, as, for example, North East England, and of the total association of features found there. Regional geography lessons aim to enable pupils to learn about the locational characteristics of one particular piece of landscape.

A recent survey identified 18 per cent of courses in secondary school, for eleven- to sixteen-year-olds, as conceptually based. 23 per cent were identified as systematically based, and 46 per cent as regionally based (D.E.S. 1974). The remaining courses were mixtures of systematic and regional courses. Earlier surveys did not identify the existence of conceptually based studies. The reasons for the development of the conceptual approach in relation to the other frameworks need to be considered at some length, for its appearance marks a significant change in school geography.

Background to change

The introduction of conceptually based studies is a product of a change in the way geographers approach the description and explanation of location.

Traditionally, geographers collected data by first-hand observation of features in the landscape. They were normally therefore concerned to study the location of tangible, recordable features. They studied the locational characteristics of things they could see or measure like rivers, climates, road networks and agricultural land use. They often stored and presented information in visual display form, on a map. Maps have the advantage of describing several types of locational information at once. They give scaled representations of absolute location, of distance and direction between features, of the pattern made by the varying locations of similar features, and of the shape of areas, for example.

Processing of information followed on from the way information was collected and the way it was described. Because geographers started with the reality of the landscape, study was inevitably set in the context of the total environment. At landscape scale, physical features dominate the scene and the impact of man almost always seemed minor and dependent. A *cause–effect model,* working outwards from the information collected, dominated physical and land–man studies. For example, particular river course patterns were seen as a product of the way in which landforms controlled the effect of fluvial processes. Process was seen as of secondary importance. A similar cause–effect *environmental determinist model* was used to study land–man relationships. This model maintained that the physical environment in some way determined human response to the landscape. The geographer therefore sought to use the information he collected to try to find the links which would explain patterns of human occupance. In particular, to do this, he used maps which allowed him to examine the areal or distributional correspondence of features. Association between features on a map was often a starting point in the search for relationships between them. Using base maps of physically defined regions fitted in well with the explanatory presupposition that the environment dominated human locational decision making. For example, transport networks and agriculture land use patterns were looked at as responses to the restraints which the physical environment imposed on man.

Working from data outwards, assuming a deterministic framework, led to much time being spent 'filling in' maps with new information and updating them. The aim was to seek fuller evidence in the hope that it would reveal ways in which the physical environment did affect locational decision making. Yet map evidence of associations never proved that any links existed. Further, most verbal explanation tended to assume there were links. Statements took the form: given the relief, climate and soils, the farming is dominated by cereal production. No necessary connections were shown between physical conditions and cereal production. Other possible variables of an economic, political or social nature were rarely mentioned except descriptively.

It became clear, however, even from map evidence, that human action can deny environmental restraints. For example, the pattern of features in the human landscape increasingly seemed to ignore physical boundaries and make nonsense of regional study based on fixed physical units. Technological advance, and the impact of particular social, economic and political attitudes on locational decision making, made the use of the deterministic model of less and less value. Better understanding of the processes of locational decision making was clearly needed if patterns were to be explained. The same need to have a greater understanding of process was apparent in physical geography also.

To solve the problem the deterministic model was replaced by the broader framework of *scientific method*, which made no assumptions about sequential cause and effect links in any one direction. This change has been described as the *conceptual revolution* in geography (Davies 1972). It is the key to an understanding of the so-called new geography in schools. It has had two important effects. One, its introduction concentrated geographical study firstly on how things came to be related locationally, and only secondly on where things are. Traditionally, geography had operated the other way round.

What is school geography?

Two, it concentrated study on seeking explanations of process in simplified model terms first. Here only a limited number of variables were looked at instead of the complexity of reality.

The procedures of scientific method, which are both *inductive* and *deductive,* allowed this new approach to develop. Instead of working almost solely from data collection towards explanation — that is, *inductively* — geographers started to use *deductive* means. That is, they started with possible explanations of how particular features came to possess distinctive locational characteristics. They then collected relevant information to see if the explanations were meaningful. To test an idea you need to spell it out precisely at the start. Otherwise you cannot assess it accurately. Care is needed to proceed logically making sure that the links in a chain of argument are clear. This is why the use of quantified data has become important in geography. Mathematics allows you to show relationships much more precisely than words.

One example of the new approach will suffice here. Supposing you wanted to try to understand the locational pattern of shops and houses in towns. You could start by mapping them in a large number of towns, or in school simply use other people's mapped evidence. A general pattern might become apparent, but the maps would never explain the pattern. Additional descriptive verbal information about the patterns would add little. The real and complex reasons for the location of shops and houses in each particular town, even if made available, might be so variably weighted that they would just obscure the key reasons for location patterns. Alternatively you could start with a simple idea about how towns are laid out, given certain assumptions. Having mastered an understanding of the idea, you could then try to see if it helps explain reality. For example, you could suppose arbitrarily, but not unreasonably, that movement by people in towns is easier to and from the centre than in any other direction, and that therefore all shopping facilities will be in the centre. This would lead you to postulate that towns would be laid out in two circles, with shops in the centre and housing around them. This model could then be used as a basis for examining reality. It is unlikely to fit perfectly because it is arbitrarily defined, and simplified, but on the basis of understanding how the simple model works, one can hopefully go on to incorporate more complex things. Deductive study of processes assumes that it is better to start with a simple idea, which is understood, rather than the complexity of reality, which is not.

Conceptual studies in schools and recent trends in the use of systematic and regional approaches start from the idea that understanding necessarily involves simplification, precise definition of terms and logical argument. The three frameworks offer different routes to this same understanding.

Conceptual studies

Of the many developments in the new geography in school, two form the basis of the conceptual approach. One is based on the identification and development of a range of ideas about location in the form of precisely defined descriptive terms. The other is based on the development of generalisations or theories which attempt to explain the locational characteristics of features.

TERMS

Many words used in geography are commonplace and have had currency in descriptive writing about landscape for a long time. Words like relief, slope and distribution are examples. Conceptually focused study aims to start by making sure pupils understand the meaning of terms like these, which geographers frequently use. A lesson which aimed to result in understanding of the word relief would hope to make it clear that the idea, or concept, contained within it appreciation of several things. For example, it contains the notion of relative height or depth, and of variation in height or depth. It also contains notions of the size and shape of a particular area of given height or depth. Further, it includes ideas on the relative locations of areas of particular height, depth, size or shape to one another. The lesson would use the same resource as a systematic or regional lesson might – for example, an Ordnance Survey map of the Castleton area of the Peak District. But the aim would not be for pupils to know about the typical relief characteristics of landforms in millstone grit or limestone, nor for them to know something about the relief of the Castleton area. It would be that they should understand the meaning of the word 'relief'. A similar approach can be adopted to develop understanding of many other words in the vocabulary of geographers.

Qualifying terms numerically Some approaches to improving definition involve giving numerical weighting to features as a matter of routine. For example, teaching approached conceptually is likely to involve giving height, areal size and slope angles to features that might normally, in the past, have been labelled simply hill, mountain, valley or plateau.

Qualifying terms genetically Other approaches for improving definition involve qualifying *generic* terms, which may be descriptive of similarity of appearance alone, like hillside slope. In this, and other comparable examples, terms are additionally defined to give some indication of how the features were formed. A *genetic* term, indicating origins or process, is used so that hillside slopes would normally be described as, for example, scree slopes or solifluction slopes. Scree slopes are a product of free-falling, loose, frost weathered material accumulating in an area, as a result of the effect of gravity. Solifluction slopes are a product of the downward creep, over permanently frozen ground below, of material lubricated by water.

Spatial terms The particular set of terms on which most work has been and is being carried out relates to *spatial structures* and *spatial processes*. They are often, again, words used widely and generally by pupils, inside and outside geography, but they are increasingly taking on more precise meaning within geography. *Spatial structures* are defined by terms which are used to indicate the arrangement of features in a landscape. They indicate the distributional characteristics of features – for example, the pattern of features. Pattern is a word which tends to be used when the distribution of points or lines is being considered, such as the sites of settlement or the road networks between them. *Spatial processes,* defined as involving movement between features, thus forming connections, have a different set of terms to describe them. Two, for example, are *agglomeration* and *dispersion,* meaning flow towards and flow away from a central point, respectively. *Connectivity,* meaning the degree of linkage of a point in a network, is another. For example, the connectivity of towns in a road network, so defined, can be given a measured weighting. Both the beta index and the cyclomatic number of a town, by slightly different summing processes, use the number of links that exist to give a measure of connectivity. Conceptual studies are then attempting to use definitions of terms to build vocabularies which will enable pupils to differentiate the locational characteristics of features more precisely.

In the series *New Ways in Geography* (Cole and Beynon 1968), one can find some of the early studies for younger secondary school pupils which are built around ideas. The contents lists of the books contain titles which are conceptually based, like 'things moving in space', 'interrupting networks', 'arranging things in patches' and 'busiest places', rather than lists of systematic features or regions. In 'busiest places' the concept is developed through the study of pupil movements past points in a school corridor, and shopper movements in a supermarket. It could equally well be derived from the study of river discharge data, however.

THEORIES

Conceptual studies try to develop an understanding of the more complex ideas contained in theories, as well as in single concepts. Teachers use both inductive and deductive approaches. There is a tendency in the inductively based studies to use simple situations like classrooms and playgrounds from which to derive initial understanding. In doing so, they are trying to take advantage of one of the features of the deductive model approach — the limitation of the number of variables considered.

Theory development Supposing you wanted to try to understand some generalisations about 'busiest places' and to develop a theory which would explain their existence. It could be approached by starting with a real life situation, or with a model or *hypothesis,* a statement of what you expect to be the case. In the real life situation, say in a school building, pupils could collect information inductively about movements of other pupils along corridors. They could space themselves at equidistant points and record the numbers of pupils who passed them during a fixed period of time. They could then bring the information together on a plan of the school marking flow lines along the corridors, proportionate to the number of pupils who passed them. From this, 'busiest places' could be identified, and a discussion could then take place as to the reasons for their location. Similar studies could be done at different times and in different places. Some generalisations about the kinds of locations that are busy could be built up.

Alternatively, using the deductive approach, they might decide, in advance, what they think the likely busiest places in the school might be. This could be based on subjective experience — for example, where they usually collide with other pupils! It could be based upon where they thought busiest places ought to be — for example, where most corridors meet. The procedure would then be to gather information about pupil movements as before, but this time deliberately using the particular points which they think are likely to be the busiest. Drawing up the information in a flow line diagram would indicate which of the points they had in mind was the busiest. Their hypothesis may, or may not, have proved correct. To refine their theory and give it wider applicability than in schools, pupils would have to work on other data and see if their theory fitted or helped explain the facts in a new situation.

Concentration here is on the development of ideas of general relevance to the study of location, as it is when terms are the focus of study. But once again particular features or particular areas can be used to assist theory development or illustrate the ideas.

This simple example of the conceptual study of 'busiest place' theory shows the type of study taking place in geography generally to develop theories about location. It is also a theory which is typical of the most coherent group of theories so far developed in geography, namely those related to *central place*. Several specific examples of the use of central place theory are now incorporated for study in public examination syllabuses. Though they are often taught in the context of studies of particular features, in systematic studies, they need not be so taught. For specific theories such as Zipf's statement of the relationship between number and size of settlement and Horton's statement on the relationship between the size of a river and the number and ordering of tributaries are conceptually similar.

Some teachers are building syllabuses around conceptual theories which are then applied to topics set in particular areas (Cromarty 1975). Texts are also appearing which aim to give 'the majority of pupils an overall framework of theory in geography' (Oxford Geography Project 1974, 1975). Both inductive and deductive approaches are in evidence.

Normative theories One particular feature of many of the theories being used in conceptual studies is important. They are theories about what *ought* to be, given certain assumptions (like the 'busiest place' theory about places where corridors meet). These theories about what ought to be, rather than what is, are called *normative* theories. They are not derived from personal experience, like colliding in the corridor. Some geography teachers, used to the traditions of first-hand field work, find it difficult to handle normative theories as the starting point for studies. They are sceptical because the ideas do not derive from empirical evidence of the real world, and feel unhappy presenting and using theories which are 'untrue'. If seen, and used explicitly, as ideas to help illuminate the real world, rather than reflect it, the problem of their use could disappear. A useful introduction to theories in geography can be found in *Geography: A Modern Synthesis* (Haggett 1972) or *Spatial Organisation: A Geographer's View of the World* (Abler, Adams and Gould 1970).

Many normative theories derive from work in the social sciences such as economics, sociology or psychology. Their use in geography is important for they have provided vehicles for discussing the impact of non-tangible features on locational decision making. For example, government social and economic policies can be stated in terms of the effect these policies should have, and then examined to see whether the intended impact on particular spatial patterns or processes has occurred. For example, the outcomes of capital injection, for land reclamation or housing redevelopment in selective areas, can be assessed meaningfully as products of government policy. A study of the location of the motor car industry which offered explanations based upon the accessibility of the manufacturing centres to raw material, as measured in route miles, or other tangible evidence alone, would not be very meaningful today.

The introduction of the use and study of normative theory has had one other effect. It has enabled geographers to handle ideas based upon value judgements, as well as on objective fact. There is a growing field of conceptually based study built upon information of people's perception of space. For example, there are classroom exercises on the concept of distance which involve pupils drawing out the length they think routes are to places from school. These are then compared with maps of the actual distance, and probably also to maps showing distance expressed as the time taken to get to the places. The concept of distance can then be seen to be dependent upon both perception and definition. A useful introduction to perception studies in general is to be found in *Mental Maps* (Gould and White 1974).

Though only 18 per cent of courses were identified as conceptually based in secondary schools in 1971–2 (D.E.S. 1974), a further survey would probably indicate that more schools now use this framework for study. It is likely that most courses are still systematic or regional, however.

Systematic studies

Systematic studies focusing on the study of the locational characteristics of particular features are found in schools in three basic forms. They exist firstly as the subdivisions of *academic systematic geography* such as physical, human and economic geography. Secondly, they feature as *thematic studies* looking at topics, such as water supply, which may bring together information from any one of the academic subdivisions. Thirdly, they feature as *concentric courses* where individual topics from within academic systematic geography are featured. For example, in concentric courses, consideration of farming locations at a given depth of study on varying scales might be followed by study of an aspect of physical geography, such as fluvial landscape formation, before returning to farming locations in greater detail, again on varying scales. The nature of these three types of study, and of changes taking place within them, is worth separate consideration.

ACADEMIC SYSTEMATIC STUDIES

Teachers and pupils will be familiar with the topics one might expect to find in contents lists of books and examination syllabuses on the subdivisions of academic geography. Looking, for example, at a list of geomorphological topics in a physical geography book would reveal titles like the Earth's crust, igneous landforms, fluvial landscapes, desert environments, glaciated landscapes, coastlines, and lakes. A list of topics in economic geography would include study of world agricultural systems and location of major extractive, manufacturing and service industries. A list of topics in human geography would include rural and urban settlements, settlement patterns, and aspects of demography.

The broad headings of topics have in fact changed very little over the last twenty years, but the approach to study within all subdivisions has changed markedly. It is, in fact, within the subdivisions of academic geography that the conceptual revolution gathered momentum. It is here that most of the specific theoretical advances were made. Similarly it is here that the significant developments in the use of particular techniques of study have taken place. Both development in theory and development in techniques found their way into schools through systematic geography in the first place.

The most apparent general trend has been the move away from the presentation of descriptive facts alone, towards the presentation of facts in the context of explanation, based upon theory. In physical geography certain aspects of scientific method had always been apparent, and direct use was made of studies of the physics of the atmosphere, the chemistry of soils and the studies of geologists and botanists. Too often, however, the rigorously argued, and often quantified, explanations of these natural sciences appeared in geography texts in the form of descriptive verbal generalisations divorced from supporting data and from the theoretical arguments which had produced them. This is less likely to be the case now, and one can expect to find equations presented which set out energy transfers in the atmosphere, diagrams which present chemical formulae, geological theories stated and the botanical names of plants used.

Descriptions of the physical environment based upon static evidence, observed and recorded around the world, are being transformed into studies which emphasise the dynamic, ever changing nature of the physical environment. Two general but related models are used to handle this emphasis on the dynamic. One is an *equilibrium model*. It is used in studies of landscape, and views them as a product of the balance of forces operating. Earlier studies were based upon a classification of landscapes in types, in relation to their stage of development, rather than the processes operating. This evolutionary model was based upon one particular interpretation of W. M. Davis's framework for landscape study, built around structure, process and time (Davis 1954). The equilibrium model focuses attention on process – for example, on the effects of channelled water flow and sheet flood on valley forms. The other general model is based upon the idea of the ecosystem, a model of ecological relationships first introduced into geography in schools through studies of vegetation. The *systems model* forms the framework for modern studies of world climate and soils as well as vegetation. This model views features as having circulatory self-regulating characteristics which maintain themselves, and change only as a result of inputs or outputs. For example, plants and vegetation associations can be seen as self-regulating systems receiving energy input via leaves and roots, and losses from seeding and tissue decay. Atmospheric and soil studies can be similarly viewed dynamically. A systems model is particularly helpful to establish the links of a chain reaction in order to show that change in one part of a system affects all the other parts by feedback.

If equilibrium and systems models dominate thinking in physical geography, analogous models feature in economic and human geography. Most of them are based on the assumption that decision making by man is rational, and that he will take into account the cost of movement. Measures and explanations of *cost–distance relationships* underpin most theories about the location of economic activity and patterns of settlement. In considering the location of heavy manufacturing industry, for example, one theory postulates that such industry will be located at a point where the raw material can be assembled at least cost. Another theory suggests that a maximum profit location is more likely. Both are built on assessments of the balance of advantage in cost–distance relationships. Many normative theories of this kind now form the starting point for studies of human and economic geography in schools.

THEMATIC STUDIES
Thematic studies, in contrast to those above, are centred around topics which require location information from several of the subdivisions of academic geography to be brought together. They often focus on the locational aspects of 'problem' features of the landscape and environment. Typical topics might be 'water and air pollution' which would require bringing together aspects of meteorology and fluvial geomorphology and uses of water and the air. Other topics might include 'The National Parks and Conservation policy' and 'land reclamation in urban, rural and coastal areas'. For example, the National Parks theme might discuss environmental quality and the reasons for initial location, accessibility by road and rail, and limits on industrial development and types of house building in United Kingdom parks. Land reclamation involves considering varying possible site uses, possible rerouting of communications, physical site factors in relation to drainage and load bearing capacity, and political decision making.

Work in this thematic style in schools tends to post-date the breakaway from the deterministic framework within which land–man relationships were previously studied. Man is firmly the point of departure in many of them. The titles of the units of the Schools Council Geography for the Young School Leaver Project illustrate the point. They are 'Man, Land and Leisure', 'Cities and People', and

'People, Place and Work' (Schools Council 1974, 1975). A variety of urban themes is particularly in evidence, reflecting the fact that this is the commonly experienced environment for a large number of pupils. Thematic studies have existed in the universities for over thirty years under the heading *applied geography*. Though they were taught courses, many of them were postgraduate and much of the work was directly research oriented. In this context geographers found themselves members of teams brought together from several areas of study. For example, in rural redevelopment programmes, geographers might find themselves working with agricultural economists, hydrologists, soil chemists and sociologists.

Many of the problems of applied geography clearly needed multidisciplinary expertise. Working in teams, so based, helped to face geographers in universities with the need to make the contribution of their subject clear. The development of multidisciplinary work in schools has grown primarily out of work on curriculum development in education in general, but in character much of it matched the approach of applied geography. School syllabuses have been built around themes to which a number of individual subjects contribute. Geographers and historians quite often find themselves working together, for example. Working in this way has faced geographers in schools, as it has in universities, with the need to make clear their particular contribution to a pupil's understanding of the world in which he lives. It has resulted in many cases in a sharper focus being placed on the study of location.

CONCENTRIC STUDIES

Some systematic studies are dominated by concern to make sure that an understanding of the locational characteristics of particular features should take into account the importance of scale. Individual topics from within systematic studies tend to be taken, and their locational characteristics examined at differing scales. For example, dairy farming in a local area might be followed by study of dairy farming on a larger scale in another part of the British Isles, and then, say, in the north island of New Zealand. A final section might look at the worldwide pattern. The next topic studied might be one from physical geography. The geographical point underlying this approach is that appreciation and understanding of locational patterns depends, in part, on scale considerations. For example, study of the siting of volcanoes in Iceland may make them appear a unique clustered feature; study of them in a group of islands, like Japan, may give the impression that they are usually linear features, while worldwide study would see them as linked along the edge of continental plates and stress zones in widely scattered locations. Pupils need to be made aware of the relationship between pattern and scale.

The approach also has general educational advantages. Pupils work from the known to the unknown. They return to similar topics at differing scales and degrees of detail, from year to year. Concentric studies first appeared some twenty-five years ago. Most texts associated with them presented straightforward descriptive information about the chosen topics and paid little attention to process. Few schools now use concentric studies in this form. Some teachers are now building their own courses, bringing together emphasis on scale and process. No attempt is made to cover all aspects of geomorphology or any other systematic section of geography. Only selected topics are studied.

Overall systematic studies are growing in schools. It is the third approach — regional studies — that has declined most, as conceptual and systematic studies have grown.

Regional studies

Study of location features, on the basis of regions which contain a complex assemblage of features, traditionally begins in school at continental scale. It is followed by studies of the individual countries within a continent, and then by study of a country's internal regions. A common syllabus sequence involves study of Africa, South America and Australia in one year, followed by North America and Asia, and then Europe, in successive years. Something resembling this pattern was found in 46 per cent of schools studied in *Education Survey No 19* (D.E.S. 1974).

It was once possible to assume that in attempting world regional coverage teachers aimed to present comparable information on every area, in a fairly set order. For example, at continental, national and then regional level, descriptions of the structure and relief of landforms would precede descriptions of climate, agriculture, industry, settlement and finally communications and trade. Within continents and countries physically contiguous units were usually considered in order. Some public examination syllabuses still tend to do little more than catalogue regions to be studied, particularly for C.S.E. and G.C.E. O level examinations. In parallel, publishers' texts contain series in which sequenced regional description is presented.

A look at examination questions, as opposed to syllabuses, and a closer look at a full range of textbooks indicates that ordered regional study is not universal. Questions in examination papers require the setting of regional studies in national contexts. They require the study of selective topics only, within particular regions. They also demand knowledge gained first hand of a local region to illustrate answers to questions set in general terms. With regard to texts, changes in books on the British Isles illustrate developments generally. Instead of working from the southeast to the north of Scotland, or vice versa in a set sequence, some texts are totally built around studying regions in so far as they illustrate particular topics of importance nationally. For example, the metropolitan county regions might be studied together as urban areas. Chapters on the Highlands of Scotland might be followed by studies of the southwest peninsula.

These, and the early contiguous regional studies, are characterised by the presentation of regional information in three forms: verbal descriptions, maps, and photographs. The emphasis in verbal description is on presenting broad generalisation about the features found together in a region. In some cases there is still a hint that the physical environment controls the total character of the region. The larger the area of study, the more this type of statement remains a feature. Maps are used, as in other styles of study, to display symbolically areal distributions and associations. Photographs provide a chance to look at a sample of the complexity of regional features.

LOCAL REGIONAL STUDIES

Additional features of many present day regional studies are worth noting. Much more emphasis is being given to study of the local landscape and the immediate region in which the school is set. Attention is often given to this in preference to complete regional coverage of the British Isles. It often involves the total exclusion of studies on some continental regions. Behind this development lies a desire to get away from gross verbal generalisation to look at specific real detail. The local region is thought most appropriate for providing this. It also allows first-hand field study.

CASE STUDIES

A second characteristic feature is, in a sense, a complementary one. A small-scale case study is often used when examining overseas regions, to allow pupils an insight into the complexity of real detail. These studies are chosen to be typical and representative of their wider region. Often case studies are presented through the eyes or lives of named individuals to give them the feeling of being real. Collections of regional case studies from all over the world have been published. One contains a study of Rosca, a village in peninsular Italy in which the village and surrounding land are viewed in terms of the life of a local farmer, Rossi Giovanni (Rushby, Bell and Dybeck 1971). This is typical of most case studies presenting a wealth of detail in words, maps, plans, data tables and photographs. Case studies have also been published within established textbook series for the last fifteen years.

REGIONS AND THE NEW GEOGRAPHY

A third feature of many regional lessons is not particularly apparent from textbooks and syllabuses. It is that teachers are using many of the significant developments from systematic geography within regional studies. This has been done by taking materials from a wide range of magazine articles, from in-service teacher workshops and from original articles and advanced texts. The basis for incorporation is that the particular materials relate to features which happen to be within the region under study in the school. Studies of the regional geography of North America have incorporated many new ideas and techniques in this way. This is because many of them were first developed or illustrated in the North American continent. For example, models of urban environments, based upon work in Chicago, have been used as frameworks for analysing the internal structure of cities in all the regions of the United States. Because, however, most work using new techniques and involving the development of explanatory theory has been carried out in the advanced industrial areas of the world, most of the examples relate to these areas. Consequently, new techniques and theories have been introduced very unevenly within regional studies in schools. For some areas of the world no studies involving new approaches have been published.

SPECIAL PURPOSE REGIONS

The traditional order of regional studies has broken down. The study of a physically based region as a unique area, within which associations between features could be described and explained successfully, is probably no longer the norm. Regional groupings used for study are frequently based on economic criteria like the European Economic Community or the Third World. Within countries, differing regional units are used to examine particular patterns and linkages, which are only meaningful outside traditionally defined regions. The urbanised coastal region of the United States, from Boston to Washington, variously styled Megalopolis or Bos-wash, would be given little coherent meaning if considered separately in the New England states, as New York and the Hudson Valley, and as settlement on the northern east coast plain – that is, within the traditional regional subdivisions of the area.

There is a tendency for traditionally organised regional studies to disappear completely in schools, rather than be revived along the lines indicated by using new techniques and theories within them. But where revived, as in conceptual and systematic studies, it is true to say that emphasis is on explaining patterns and processes of relative location rather than simply describing absolute locations.

It is a healthy sign for geography teaching that the views discussed above are the subject of lively debate in geography teachers' magazines, as well as within school geography departments. Ideally many teachers would like to offer courses to pupils which, at differing times, use all of the three basic styles discussed. Whatever the balance of choice by any individual teacher, it is likely that a clearer view of the understanding of spatial patterns and processes of location will result. Pupils can be seen to have benefited from the critical look at the nature of geography which has taken place during the last fifteen years.

2 How is geography learnt?

Formal learning in schools is built around activities by pupils, on the basis of studies prepared and organised by teachers. Approaching geography in terms of pupil learning activities is useful, for teacher activity in itself cannot promote learning. Further, the effectiveness of pupil learning is the only real measure of successful teaching.

Discussion of the nature of geography in schools will have suggested already that pupils are likely to be involved in a wide range of activities. In the classroom, and in the field, the variety of forms in which evidence of location might be available indicates that a number of techniques and skills will be needed to collect evidence. Similarly, the processing of information and its critical assessment are likely to require several styles of procedure, considerable understanding and sound judgement. The role of the geography teacher is to pick out and plan the use of those activities which will serve the learning of geography most effectively.

Types of learning

In order to do this, it is helpful to try to distinguish the major kinds of activity in learning in general. One way of bringing order to the many possible learning activities is to divide them into categories, based upon similarity of purpose. On this basis it is possible to distinguish three kinds of activity. They are those associated with the acquisition of skills, those associated with the learning of different levels of knowledge, and those associated with the development of attitudes (Bloom 1956, Krathwohl 1964). It would not serve the purpose of this chapter to look at all possible strategies under these headings. Readers must accept that the whole range of approaches to learning in education, in general, could be incorporated into planned lessons by geography teachers. Some appear to play a particular part in promoting geographical learning to advantage, and these will be highlighted under the headings of skill acquisition, knowledge learning, and attitude development.

Skill acquisition

Logically this deserves first consideration. For all learning activities involve two things. One is data recording via the senses. The other is the coordination and processing of this sense perception via the brain. How learning actually takes place remains a mystery, despite the considerable advances made by research into neurophysical and chemical structures. Bloom and his colleagues described a sequence of types of knowledge learning and attitudinal development, but though they distinguished skill acquisition separately they did not describe any general sequence of types of skill acquisition. Broadly, however, skill acquisition relates to those activities which involve developing the coordinated use of the senses and body movements. As implied earlier, effective pupil learning, in general, requires successful coordination of all the senses. It is, however, to visual observation and hand–eye coordination that geographers pay particular attention.

VISUAL OBSERVATION
Observation of location, at landscape scale, requires dominantly visual skills, beyond simply possession of the ability to see. Given sight, skill development involves being able to read visual signals of light and shade, colour and form, in such a way as to be able to identify and differentiate location data.

Thus, from an early stage, pupils in geographical studies would be encouraged to note that features possess locational properties, by being asked where something which they can see is – for example, the teacher's desk in a classroom. The work of the psychologist Piaget and his associate (Piaget and Inhelder 1956), describing children's perceptions of space, has been of very considerable importance in aiding geography teachers' understanding of how children perceive space. The recent book, *The Child's Discovery of Space* (Sauvy and Sauvy 1974), offers some stimulating thoughts on ways in which geographers might structure work involving the development of visual observation skills by younger children.

By practising visual discriminatory skills, pupils can progressively build up and refine their perception of locations. Piaget described three types of space perception systems and maintained that they developed sequentially. The initial possession of sight allows the process of differentiation to begin early in a child. Things are perceived as being close or far away in relation to one's person. At a later stage, with appropriate encouragement, children perceive locations in terms of direction, as well as of distance. Things are in front, behind, above, below, to the left and to the right. Both distance and direction still use self as a reference point. A second stage of development, which can be built up and refined within the early years of formal education, involves learning to perceive objects in relation to each other, and not only to oneself. The questions 'How far is it between two objects?' and 'What is the direction of one object from another?' require the ability to perceive distance and direction. At a third stage, children begin to perceive things in terms of arbitrary coordinate systems and can locate things in relation to a matrix of lines, not directly dependent upon particular objects.

Clearly there is a narrow line dividing perception from conception. The former may be defined here as involving sensory data collection and associated initial learning. Conception implies that the memory has assimilated the data. Children can then make use of, and probably explain, that which has been perceived. In the context of work in junior and middle schools, developing visual skills to assist description of location is a basic activity. By using simple environments, like the classroom, and small-scale real space outside in playgrounds, children can be involved in developing their visual skills through all stages, until they can handle all three conceptual systems without difficulty. Exercises involving linking up and ordering themselves in lines in the playground, pacing distances between things, using walls as direction lines and playing games involving numbering spaces, are simple examples. The geographer will want to tie up the development of a realistic visual perception of space with making a representation of it.

HAND–EYE COORDINATION

At the earliest stage in junior school work, representations of relative location on paper are often built around encouraging pupils to draw 'my route from classroom to playground', for example. This would involve taking the piece of paper out along the route and drawing in the stages from direct visual observation, one by one. From drawing up visually estimated short distances and relative directions, without reference to scale or measurement of angles, the child can progress through a sequence of activities. Measurement can be introduced, as can the need for scale. This will involve learning to handle simple measuring devices and to observe distances accurately against them. Original map making activities can be refined and developed until, at G.C.E. A level, trigonometrical surveying equipment might be used in the field to make accurate maps of areas of considerable size. A slightly different range of activities is involved in learning to coordinate hand and eye, so as to be able to draw outline maps free hand. It involves accurate perception of the relative spacing of points and lines, so that the shape of areas can be drawn successfully. Free-hand map drawing activities are quite often built into the early years of secondary school geography lessons.

The development of visual observation skills and associated hand–eye coordination skills have been claimed as a particular responsibility which teachers of geography should shoulder, because of their close relationship to map making and simple map reading. The term 'graphicate' skills is sometimes used to describe them (Balchin 1972). From the basic activities of the junior school, and early secondary school, much more complex visual skills are developed.

ADVANCED VISUAL SKILLS

In geography, in the field and in the classroom pupils have to handle increasingly complex visual data. Sketching skills need to be developed if, for example, pupils are to attempt to analyse in the field the component parts of a physical landscape, covering a large area. Similarly, this is true if they have to analyse oblique, aerial or vertical photographs in the classroom. Field sketching techniques do not develop without learning visual identification of the key perspective lines in a landscape, and practising drawing. Effective visual reading skills need developing in relation to photographs. Apart from making use of natural perspective lines to break up a photograph for study, deliberate controlled rather than random scanning techniques need to be learnt to achieve complete data sensing.

In some respects the ability to recall information in visual terms – for example, remembering landscape scenes 'in the mind's eye' – may represent a fairly high order outcome of the development of visual skills. Certainly the development of a sense of location seems to require geographers to teach visually based skills.

Knowledge learning

Learning can take place at a number of levels. A pupil may simply be able to learn and remember information but little else, or he may be able to show an understanding of it beyond the simple ability to recall it. A number of attempts have been made to identify and classify different levels of understanding. The classification adopted by Bloom used the headings *knowledge, comprehension, application, analysis, synthesis,* and *evaluation,* the simplest being knowledge recall and the most complex being evaluation. Activities at higher levels incorporate understanding at all the lower levels. This framework is used by a considerable number of geography teachers for planning lessons and preparing assessments of pupil learning.

An example, taken from one possible sequence of learning, will make the distinctions within the classification clear. The von Thünen agricultural land use model postulates that, other things being equal, given the existence of a single central town in which to market produce, circular zones of differing agricultural land use would represent the most economic use of the land. A pupil may learn this model in the form of a diagramatic representation of it, as circles drawn around a point. Each circle might be labelled with the name of a particular type of farming. Simple ability to recall this diagram, and reproduce it in the same form as the original, would indicate that the pupil had *knowledge* of it. If, on the other hand, not having previously learnt alternative descriptions by rote, he could then transform the diagram, and present it in graph form to show the relationship between distance from the centre point and type of land use, he would have demonstrated that he could claim *comprehension* of the model.

A higher level of understanding would be demonstrated if the pupil could use the model in a novel situation, and illustrate the relevance of it to help explain mapped land use patterns as they exist around particular market towns. This would demonstrate that *application* of the model was possible by the pupil. Further understanding involving analysis would be displayed, if the pupil examined the model critically in such a way that he could point out that the model effectively handles only one variable, the effect of distance from market on land use, whereas other variables are involved in land use zonation. For example, he could point out that the physical parameters of the environment are not uniform, as postulated. The development of a new diagram of the model, by the pupil, which incorporated the influence of variation of relief, for example, would demonstrate understanding at the level of *synthesis*. That is, it would demonstrate his ability to bring together old and new ideas in a new presentation. He might go further than developing new elaborations of the model and come to question the basis upon which it was constructed in the first place. For example, he might argue that the cultural or historical context in which the model was developed no longer exists in contemporary society, so that the model is invalid. This would constitute *evaluation* of the model. The framework provided by this classification of levels of knowledge, as illustrated above, will help to highlight particular characteristics and trends in how cognitive understanding contributes to learning in geography.

KNOWLEDGE

Remembering information presented in a variety of forms — for example, as spoken or written words, data tables or maps — constitutes a part of most geographical studies. Rote learning is usually employed to aid recall in this way. The simple learning and recall of lists of 'capes and bays' or economic products tends to have disappeared, and knowledge for the sake of knowledge is given less importance than in the past. Activities tend to be organised for pupils which involve higher levels of understanding and incorporate knowledge learning within them.

The emphasis is on helping pupils to gain access to knowledge stored in books, atlases and reference systems of all kinds. Factual knowledge is increasingly seen as something to be gained initially from storage systems, at the point at which it needs to be used. It is not necessarily always to be stored in a pupil's memory. This is reflected in geography lessons which are increasingly resource rich. Geographers are dealing with resource information about locations which can become out of date and meaningless very rapidly. The facility to forget useless knowledge could be said to be as important as the ability to retain useful knowledge.

COMPREHENSION

Cultivation of understanding of knowledge, in use in activities, is a different matter. By developing comprehension, teachers make sure that meanings are understood by individuals and incorporated into their learning procedures. This implies that there should be no need for reference back to an initial knowledge resource, at least while the term, procedure or idea is actively in use by the pupil.

Methods of promoting comprehension and assessing it are probably better developed in geography now than ever before, because data are now used in a wider variety of formats than in the past. Numerically presented data, say on the weather, can be converted into linear or bar graph form. Landform sketches can be made from photographs. Verbal descriptions can be written on diagrammatically presented information, say on settlement patterns. Oral summaries using tape recorders can be made of written paragraphs or directly observed features, say of traffic flow. The presentation of oral information by a teacher and its recall and representation in oral form, and the presentation of written work, based on reading books, were less effective devices for promoting comprehension than exercises requiring transformation of data.

Probably many school subjects are trying to make a better job of promoting comprehension by methods like those illustrated. In relation to map work geographers are making one particular contribution. It involves mapping space in alternatives to real linear scale terms – for example, substituting scales showing the times taken travelling between places rather than the distance between them in kilometres. Another example is transforming maps so that they show the connections between places clearly, while not showing true distances or true relative positions. The London Underground map is an example of this. The use of world maps representing countries by size according to their populations or gross national product per head, instead of areal size, is another example. Perhaps in geography, more than in other subjects, pupils are involved in activities involving visual transformations of data which require comprehension.

APPLICATION

Use of knowledge which is comprehended represents a higher level of understanding than those considered so far. Two features in geography teaching will illustrate ways in which this kind of learning is being promoted.

One is a product of the increasing use of concepts and theories as starting points for study. Given comprehension of a theory, application to real life situations follows. For example, Christaller's theoretical distribution of settlements in hexagonal patterns can be used to study settlement distributions shown on Ordnance Survey maps. When dealing with links between features, at very different scales, during the course of study, application of theory is a particularly illuminating approach to study.

A second recent feature relates to assessment procedures in geography. Increasingly, assessment deliberately emphasises the need for a pupil to be able to apply his knowledge to new situations, rather than simply to recall known knowledge orally or verbally. Data response questions, as they are called, are now appearing in public examinations. They feature more frequently in normal classwork also. All the specific facts needed are given to a pupil in the question. The problem for the pupil is to apply his understanding of them to answer the questions.

ANALYSIS

Analysis involves being able to break down information into discrete parts so that they can be distinguished separately, and relations between the parts and the whole can be understood. One of the traditional analytic activities in geography involves pupils in map analysis. A very simple exercise would involve pupils taking separate tracings of individual features from a topographical map, and then examining relationships by matching tracings in pairs, for example. By removing the 'noise' created by the complexity of a multipurpose map, the connections between parts can be made more clear, at least visually. The maze of roads and contour lines on some maps may make comprehension of relations between them difficult. Mapping A roads, B roads and others separately, and comparing them with a tracing of relief contours could be the beginning of a precise exercise relating kilometre lengths of types of road to certain heights, for example.

If this is a fairly typical analytical activity involving visual data, one of the developments in recent years, hinted at in the last example, involves the increasing use of quantitative data. Mathematics and mathematical statistics have offered means of effective analysis which the verbal analysis of qualitative data did not. Quantified representation of the pattern of energy transfer in the atmosphere, or of relationships in a food chain, make meaningful analysis much easier for pupils. Imprecise verbal generalisation did not permit effective analysis. Number not only offers precise statements of size, but allows orders of magnitude to be established. Mathematical statistics offer techniques for looking at probabilities in relation to associations between features as indicated by deviations from standard norms, rank order and coefficient measures. Two simple examples illustrating mathematical analysis of geographical location data follow. One, correlation graphs showing rainfall and crop growth in different locations can be used to show trend lines, which would indicate positive or negative relationships. Two, rank orders of correlation can be worked out using Spearman's Rank Correlation Coefficient, for example, to establish relationships between incomes per head of urban population and motor car ownership. More precise analysis of this kind characterises current developments in school geography.

SYNTHESIS

Both map making and the writing of local regional geography can be creative synthetic activities for pupils. The studies which probably involve synthetic understanding most effectively take place when pupils are carrying out individual or small group field work activities in a limited area. It is then possible to face a pupil with a task that is sufficiently limited in scale to be attainable. In a given length of time, having limited objectives, a pupil can sustain an interest in the task. Map making and the writing of local regional geography are typical examples of synthetic work and feature as possible parts of individual projects in several C.S.E. and G.C.E. syllabuses, where continuous assessment procedures are used. More work of this kind is appearing at all levels in school.

Theoretical frameworks, whether descriptive or explanatory, help pupils to see and express connections. One in particular, general systems theory, is a helpful vehicle for pupils trying to present studies of locational patterns and processes. For it is a universal model capable in principle of handling very complex data. Its full potential has yet to be realised in school geography though specific applications have been mentioned earlier.

EVALUATION

Work requiring effective critical judgement, or justification of the validity of an argued case, represents the highest level of understanding in Bloom's hierarchy.

Internal criteria. Judgements of internal truth or value, within a statement, are required when the relevance of a concept or theory about location in geography is considered. Learning in geography has advanced considerably in this respect because of the use of scientific method and particularly of deductive reasoning. The methods of science have brought a sharper edge to intellectual activity at this level. Pupils expect arguments to be logically consistent and coherent. By using scientific method they are trained to incorporate critical standards into their thinking, as never before.

External criteria and the use of simulation. Perhaps the most significant development of note relates, however, to ways in which pupils are now often taught to handle external criteria when making judgements. The learning device employed, virtually unknown in geography teaching fifteen years ago, is simulation. Simulation is largely associated with the study of human locational decision making. It usually involves the pupils in role-playing the part of a decision maker. Within simplified fixed constraints and rules, the pupils are asked to carry out a set of procedures. These, stage by stage, involve the pupil in using his personal judgement, basing his decisions upon the evidence available and his own view of it. For example, a pupil may, as an individual activity, be asked to plan a road stretching across an area, knowing that it has to reach a certain destination. Information about construction costs per unit of land crossed may be simply related to height of relief, for example. But usually the pupil is presented with incomplete information. What can be calculated fairly easily as the cheapest route to construct may have hazards marked along it. The pupil then has to decide whether to take this route and chance the effect of the information which will be revealed when he reaches the point or whether to avoid it. Several variably located hazards would pose considerable decision making problems.

Simulation can be much more sophisticated than this. Many activities involve groups of pupils competing against one another to achieve the 'best' results. A chance or random element is often involved, by using a dice, to give varying advantage to pupils round by round. These simulations take the style of games. Some simulations involve cooperative activity, when pupils act as teams of decision makers responsible for offering advice on particular aspects of locational decision making. They then have to reach a common decision, and proceed on the basis of that. At least fifty published studies are available and many teachers have developed simple simulation exercises of their own. A bibliography in the *Classroom Geographer* (Stopp 1973) is a very useful guide to the range available. It is in the context of learning critical evaluation that they have their part to play in geographical learning. Perhaps the most important styles of simulation involve studying locational decisions for which there is no 'best' answer. For then, not only during but also even at the end of the simulation, the meaning of the outcome depends upon a pupil's point of view. Studies of population dispersal across areas, or of alternative uses of locations, say coastal areas, are of this kind. *Games in Geography* (Walford 1969) was an early publication which makes the role of simulation clear.

Planning and organising the learning of knowledge in geography is identifiably more complex, challenging and exciting for teachers than in the past. But they have to recognise that it is not only skills and knowledge that are being acquired, but also attitudes.

Attitude development

Teachers of geography, like other teachers in our society, tend to be reluctant to appear directly involved in developing pupil attitudes in a way which might affect the value which pupils subsequently place on things. Indirect influence is usually acknowledged, but is regarded as inevitable and unconscious.

However, if pressed, teachers and pupils alike would probably agree that teachers are clearly and directly involved in at least two respects, though neither of them relate to the value that might be placed on the subject being studied. Firstly, they are involved in affecting pupils' general behaviour in schools, so that the pupils will value the circumstances in which learning can take place. Secondly, they are concerned that pupils should value the particular methods of learning or techniques which will enable them to cope successfully with studies. The inculcation of attitudes to behaviour and learning generally pose teachers, as a group, with few problems. It is in relation to matters of value judgement and belief that contentious issues arise.

To look at how geography teachers are involved in the development of attitudes by pupils, it is helpful to use the framework mentioned at the beginning of the chapter (Krathwohl 1964). This is based upon identification of levels of acceptance of values by pupils. That is, on how far the pupil internalises a value and uses it as his own. The broad categories identified were labelled *receiving, responding, valuing, organisation,* and *characterisation by a value or value complex*. Receiving and responding can be looked at, and explained together. The remaining three will be similarly grouped here.

RECEIVING AND RESPONDING

At the levels of receiving information and responding to it, teachers are really concerned with pupil motivation. The degree of interest pupils take in learning, and learning geography in particular, clearly does matter. Geography teachers need to take account of attitudinal development at this level.

To promote initial awareness which evokes willing response is by no means easy. One device used is to present pupils with apparent problems or unusual information which may rouse their curiosity. Both devices are widely used by teachers of many subjects. Geographical studies of location offer many opportunities to begin lessons in this way. It might even be argued, rather unfairly, that so much about location remains unresolved, and the world offers so many unusual features located outside the environment which most children experience, that geography teachers should have no difficulty in motivating pupils.

One interesting feature of the Schools Council Geography 14—18

Project was that it used a set of mis-match problems in its trial schools, as examples of ways of motivating pupils to take an interest in geographical topics. A particular example is worth examination. It presented, without comment, a Reuter report quoted in *The Guardian*, describing how a Swiss tourist couple on holiday in Hongkong took their pet poodle with them one day into a restaurant. 'They asked a waiter over to their table and pointed to the poodle while they made eating motions, to show that they wanted it to be fed. There was some difficulty communicating with the waiter they said, but eventually he took the dog into the kitchen under his arm.' After some delay the waiter returned with their main dish. 'When they picked up the silver lid they found their poodle roasted inside, garnished with pepper sauce and bamboo shoots.' It was reported that the Swiss couple left for Zurich hurriedly, much disturbed.

This type of starter could bring considerable reaction from the pupils. In terms of receiving and responding, most pupils would certainly pay attention and listen to such a story. They would ask if it were true. They would probably want to seek for an explanation from the teacher or from books. It might lead them on to want to know much more about Chinese cultural traditions, as well as, in particular, their attitude to dogs. They might want to analyse how the situation came to occur. Probably, however, they would have to go beyond receiving and responding to this story about culture clash caused by people moving from one location to another and begin to argue about whether anyone was to blame for the incident. Here, value judgements come into play.

VALUING AND ORGANISING VALUE SYSTEMS

If an oral debate followed in class, pupils would probably display a variety of views about the Swiss, tourists, the Chinese, dogs, and the advisability of going to foreign locations. How should a teacher handle situations involving value judgements?

Approaches to explicit discussion of values. Some would argue that he should simply give an opportunity for pupils to express their views and act as a strictly neutral chairman. Whether very partial or a balanced range of views are offered, his role is to be silent. Others would argue that he should try to make pupils aware that there are possible alternative views held. He would then put these alternatives to balance an argument, though they may not be his own personal views. A third approach would be for the teacher to join in a debate as though he were one of a number of equals, and put his own view. A fourth approach would be to put his own view, and directly assert that all the other views are incorrect. Geography teachers are known to adopt all these approaches from time to time.

In relation to the specific case of the restaurant incident, I might feel that it would be appropriate not to be neutral, but promote the view that the Swiss and the Chinese points of view should both receive fair consideration. I might go further, and encourage a wider view that all people's attitudes should be examined seriously as possible alternatives to one's own. I might ultimately want my pupils to internalise this attitude, as a general view, which they held permanently so that they always saw locational decision making in a cultural context.

One might argue that study of other people's problems, of other people's locational decision making, in a balanced fashion is all too easy. But discussing live local issues about motorway routing, slum clearance, the siting of travellers' camps or industrial development of holiday resort coasts, if you live in the area concerned, is a different matter. In the context of local issues pupils' views are likely to be fairly firmly internalized. Should the geography teacher here simply make sure that the background facts are known or go further? My own preference here would be for the presentation of the facts, the alternative views, and my own as one of them.

Live local issues may not occur in a pupil's school lifetime, but pupils later in life may well come across issues which do involve them in making judgements about where a particular development should take place. By use of simulation, mentioned earlier as a means of learning evaluation, geography teachers have a device through which children can practise making judgements without having to face actual pay-offs.

Values presented implicitly Discussion or presentation of issues involving value judgements often takes place much less directly than in the cases mentioned. Sometimes courses or approaches assume attitudes, and fail to discuss them critically. Some courses on themes associated with pollution or conservation, for example, can easily affect pupils' subsequent attitudes, without the concepts implicit in the words ever being challenged. Some pupils who learn economic geography, in terms of the economic products of other areas which are used in Britain, can pick up, incidentally, selective attitudes to other countries and societies. The 'geography of the breakfast table' which brings together butter from Denmark, tea from India, grain from Canada, and orange juice from South Africa can leave some pupils believing that these societies exist to serve our needs. There is also, sometimes, still a tendency to want to highlight contrasts around the world rather than highlight universals. Books with titles implying that geography is the study of strange people in foreign lands have disappeared from schools. But study of both relict and past cultures exists, as though they were representative of contemporary ways of life in some areas. The environmental determinist still stalks the east African plain with the Maasi, herding cattle, and follows the Eskimo as a nomadic dweller living in igloos and tents in northern Canada. There is potentially as much danger in presenting out-of-date information as presenting particular value judgements. Pupils assimilate attitudes from both.

It is not only the nature of geography, but how it is learnt, that presents great challenges and exciting possibilities to teachers.

3 Where does geography stand in the curriculum?

Changes in the nature of geography and the way it is taught have been paralleled by changes in geography's place in the total school curriculum. Traditionally geography appears on a school timetable as one of a list of distinct subjects which will include English, history and mathematics, for example. This was once true of nearly all secondary schools, and of the timetables of upper forms in junior schools. It is no longer the case. As reported in *Education Survey No 19* (D.E.S. 1974), 90 per cent of secondary schools timetabled geography for some age groups as a separate subject. 29 per cent of the secondary schools also ran courses in which combined studies involving geography teachers was timetabled. In junior schools, geography existed as a separate subject in only 19 per cent. In the remaining junior schools it featured within or as part of combined studies, if it featured at all.

Influences on change

Influences which have brought about this change stem from the contributions psychologists, sociologists and philosophers have made to curriculum development work in schools in general. Broadly the shift has been towards using curriculum designs which are child-centred, emphasising that the child's natural perception of the world is unitary rather than fragmented. It has been reflected in organising learning so that the child takes a more active part in deciding what he should study, and the pace at which he should study. It has also been reflected, particularly in junior schools, in a shift towards using the whole of school time in an integrated way, without time units on specific days being allocated to particular subjects. This has involved staff working together more closely in teams for planning and teaching purposes. It has involved preparing work for children on a more individual and less on a whole class basis.

Combined studies

Combined studies involving geography teachers features in schools in three forms. In one form geography is retained on a timetable and regarded, because of one view of its nature, as a combined study in itself. In a second form combined studies appears in the timetable and geography does not. Here titles such as social studies, humanities, environmental studies, local studies and world studies appear instead. Usually the combined studies involve integrated team teaching. The geographer contributes to an understanding of the locational aspects of the features under study. In the third form combined studies appears under headings similar to those above (environmental studies, etc.). But in this case the headings indicate a timetable block during which, either in parallel or at separate points in the year, different subjects make a separate contribution. This type of combined study can be labelled interdisciplinary study. A look at all three separately will make geography's place in the curriculum clear.

GEOGRAPHY AS A COMBINED STUDY

There are secondary schools where this view of geography is maintained. There are unlikely to be any junior schools where this is so. Where it is maintained it is likely that the curriculum consists entirely of separate subject studies. Geography is seen to be of necessity a combined study.

It is not difficult to see how the case can be argued. Geographers, potentially, are concerned with the locational characteristics of all features at or near the Earth's surface. It is therefore a most convenient general subject in schools. It needs to draw upon other subjects to describe what features are. It uses evidence derived, in part, from other subjects, to explain how they came to be as and where they are. It draws upon evidence from the humanities, like history, to describe the development and growth of human features at particular locations. It draws upon the sciences to describe and explain physical features of the landscape. Geography lessons can act as a bridge which brings the humanities, the social and the natural sciences together. In an increasingly crowded timetable, the use of a certain amount of economics, sociology or politics in geography lessons saves having to consider the possibility of them as new separately timetabled subjects.

This undifferentiated view of geography as a general collection of facts about the world has gained and maintained credence in some schools where geographers have failed to make the central concern of geography — an understanding of location — really clear. As hinted in the discussion of features of both systematic and regional geography, heavy emphasis on description rather than explanation gave geography lessons this appearance. If, for example, geography lessons on the artificial fibre textile industry in Lancashire were prepared to present the history of the slave trade and of cotton plantations in the southern United States, and the technology of the processes of cloth making in the factories, why introduce combined studies as a new category?

The discussion of the nature of geography in chapter 1 does not sustain geography's role as a combined study of this kind. But similar views of geography continue to exist, inside and outside schools. The Schools Council Integrated Studies Project appeared to see geography only as a means of integrating other subjects for study. The Schools Council *Working Paper 39* (1971) described geography as 'the interdisciplinary subject par excellence'. But if geography is primarily the study of location, it cannot be primarily the integrated and interdisciplinary study for all aspects of all features as well. It can integrate with other subjects to study features, or contribute as one study among others focusing separately on features. It must, however, do this on the basis of the distinct contribution which it has to make itself.

Geography teachers sometimes fear that combined studies courses are taking over all their work, and that geography will disappear. It might well rather be that, if geography ceased to appear to be the only combined study in a school, it would be greatly strengthened.

GEOGRAPHY IN INTEGRATED STUDIES

It will be most helpful to look at particular integrated groupings which feature geography, one by one.

Social studies. Geography has played its part in a variety of styles of integrated social studies courses. They are usually all concerned with aspects of the study of human society. Some focus on man as an individual. Some focus on his role as the member of a family or kinship group. Others relate particularly to an individual's association with an occupational or interest group. Yet others relate to an individual and his place in society, as the national of a particular state, or as a citizen of the world.

Several examples will illustrate how geographical insights may be pooled with contributions from other subjects in such a way that there is not, in the classroom, any necessary attempt to make it clear that distinct subjects are contributing to the study. The study of man as an individual might, particularly in work with younger children, be built around themes of human endeavour. These might be linked to the lives of named individuals who were distinguished discoverers in medicine, explorers, or pioneers in social reform, or they might be linked to the varying life styles of individuals in contrasting environments. Geographical information would play its part alongside historical and sociological information to bring such topics alive. The story of several major advances in medicine would involve discussion of the exotic origins of the plants from which drugs used to improve the human condition were extracted.

An occupationally focused study might be built around careers and job opportunities locally. This could involve discussion of the role of social security services in our society. It might involve industrial visits and raise questions as to how particular industries came to be in the locality. Some older style social studies courses focused on an individual's place in society, through a study of 'civics'. That is, they focused on the administrative and bureaucratic functioning of society at a local level. Geographical content might be included in the discussion of local authority boundaries, and the distribution and accessibility of public service buildings. There is an obvious place for historical information about social and political change here also. Studies of styles of family grouping, from the nuclear to the extended, in widely contrasting environments could well be illuminated by geographical information.

Humanities If combined studies labelled 'social studies' involves sociological, historical and geographical information, humanities courses are usually more broadly based. One would normally expect aspects of work on communication through language and literature, and discussion of moral issues to play a part.

Several of the themes of the Schools Council Humanities Project such as 'War and Society' and 'Poverty, Law and Order' are of this kind. The Schools Council General Studies Project has been working on curriculum development for older pupils, but in a similar set of areas. All the humanities projects which *Education Survey No 19* (D.E.S. 1974) found being used in schools, and to which geographers were contributing, were based on one of the Schools Council national projects. No doubt, however, curriculum development has developed further in schools and additional resources and themes from outside have been added to the original starter resources. It is not necessary to labour the point that geography has a contribution to make in the study of humanities – an obvious example is the link between war and the control of terrestrial space.

Environmental studies Environmental studies has been defined in a wide variety of ways. At the broadest level it has been described as concerned with 'the relations between man, his culture and his physical surroundings' (Schools Council 1975). The leaflet which uses this definition notes examples of curriculum projects which contribute to environmental education. They include Engineering Science, Social Education, Mathematics for the Majority Continuation Project, and Design and Craft Education. They also include three projects with the word geography in their titles. It is perhaps no wonder that, among all the types of combined studies developing in schools, studies labelled 'environmental education' leave room for greatest debate about their nature. *Education Survey No 19* (D.E.S. 1974) noted that several 'environmental studies' courses, to which geographers contributed in schools, contained no scientific elements and no studies of the physical environment.

The practical development of these courses in schools seems to stem from two particular initiatives, though teachers may have drawn on resources from a large number of subject areas. Both pick up strands which are long established in the curriculum. One stems from rural science, and later rural studies, strengthened by the development of ecological studies. Interestingly, Keele University was the setting for the first 'Countryside in 1970' conference which brought teachers interested in the rural environment together. Since then, C.S.E. and G.C.E. O and A level courses have developed. Their syllabuses cover 'a study of the countryside landscape, soils; the plants and animals naturally present, their ecological relationships; the effect of man's activities, particularly farming and forestry, with an emphasis on land use and conservation' (Carson 1971). A geographer's contribution to this type of environmental study will be clear enough. It is to concentrate on locational issues.

The second initiative stems from the Schools Council Environmental Studies Project. It has been defined as an educational approach rather than in terms of a contents list. It is teaching and learning based upon direct experience of the environment. It is 'the area that can be used by the teacher as an immediate direct teaching resource' (Schools Council 1970). The comments made about ways of learning through direct visual observation and hand–eye coordination in chapter 2 will make it obvious how geographers can contribute to studies of the total local environment.

Local studies In practice there is hardly likely to be any gap between what pupils actually do on an environmental studies course, as defined immediately above, and courses which happen to be labelled local studies. In fact where geography is integrated, as many schools had local studies as environmental studies courses, according

Where does geography stand in the curriculum? 43

to *Education Survey No 19* (D.E.S. 1974). Again, just as in many combined courses, geography and history are likely to provide the key approaches to illuminate these studies. This is especially true of work undertaken by younger pupils involving mapping land use, recording building materials, age of houses, and traffic flows, for example.

World studies Clearly we are here concerned with combined studies at the opposite end of the scale to local studies. Relatively few schools have adopted this title for integrated courses. They appear, as many combined courses do, to use historical and geographical information. Quite often they are based upon studies of regions of the world with contrasting cultures – cultures which have sustained themselves over long periods of history and are thriving today.

For example, using what is a case study approach, pupils look at societies at different points in time and examine the continuities and changes. Studies of the Islamic world and of Chinese civilisation are examples. By drawing parallels with our own society, the intention is to emphasise the common features of humanity which bind us, rather than point up the contrasts. A geographer's role within those studies would again be to offer insights into spatial patterns and processes.

GEOGRAPHY IN INTERDISCIPLINARY STUDIES

Rather than examine again, separately, every one of the forms of combined study just considered under integrated studies, this section will point out, with illustrations, the way in which interdisciplinary studies contrast with integrated studies. When social studies, humanities, environmental studies, local studies and world studies are approached in an interdisciplinary fashion, the fact that a geographer is about to make a specifically geographical study is made explicit. Often it is by teaching a separately timetabled unit on the geography of a topic. The same topic is then studied separately by historians or sociologists or English teachers, or other specialists as appropriate.

An interdisciplinary study approach to a world study area might involve three separate terms' work. For example, a study of China might involve one term's study of medieval China by a historian, one term on the contemporary geography of China, and one term on contemporary Chinese society by a sociologist. Parallel studies can also take place. For example, in a local study for older pupils, lessons organised by historians, geographers and sociologists might run in parallel but be taught separately.

In distinguishing integrated and interdisciplinary studies one is, of course, sharpening a division which can be blurred in practice in many ways. For example, it is quite common to have lead lessons or lectures which set the objectives of a course before the pupils in an integrated fashion. Teachers are likely to have met together and planned their courses with complete awareness of the other elements in mind. A few specifically interdisciplinary resources have in fact been published. The series The Developing World is probably the one with which geography teachers will be most familiar. Separate but parallel books have been published on geography, history, religious instruction and science. The geography titles are *Man Alone, Living Together, A New Man,* and *Man Organizes* (Crawford 1970–2). One example of the interdisciplinary nature of these studies will suffice. In *Man Alone* pupils in geography lessons study simple and often primitive contemporary societies around the world – for example, Amazonian Indians. The historian is looking separately at the development of agricultural societies since prehistoric times. In religious studies pupils look at primitive tribal beliefs. In science they look at the origins of human life and the beginnings of man's use of his environment.

Other trends

Several other combinations of geography and established school subjects are beginning to develop. None of them is, as yet, as established as those described above, but they are worth noting.

URBAN STUDIES

One is urban studies, a specific type of local study but with origins in the social sciences, far removed from the environmental local studies, which has scientific and rural origins. Its development has been catalysed by the interest taken by the Town and Country Planning Association in fostering pupils' interest in the built environment. A Council for Urban Study Centres has been established. The Association publishes *The Bulletin of Environmental Education* and *Town Trail*. Two of its education officers have published *Streetwork: The Exploding School* (Ward and Fyson 1973). The very considerable interest of geographers in the internal structures of cities has been pointed out earlier, so the involvement of geographers cannot come as a surprise. As an integrated study, it has one other characteristic worth noting: the potential for direct involvement in arguing contrary points of view and developing attitudes is great. Urban studies can present the opportunity for closing the gap which sometimes exists between school studies and the real world, between the classroom and the street. Its advocates see schools as a base from which to go out to be educated, rather than as a centre of learning.

EARTH SCIENCES

A very different trend can be observed in the growing association of geography and the natural sciences grouped as the Earth sciences. In exploring the interfaces between physics, chemistry, biology and geology, themes and issues with spatial dimensions (at geographical scale) have become the focus of integrated study. The distribution and spread of diseases, atmospheric pollution, tidal energy, and earthquake destruction, are possible themes in Earth science studies.

4 When is geography learnt?

It will be apparent from the nature of geography and the variety of ways in which learning takes place that not all children within the school age range could possibly hope to understand the content of lessons if geography was presented to all age groups in the same way.

Guiding principles for content selection

Geographers have adopted a number of general patterns for sequencing learning, commonly used in other subjects also. Usefully four can be identified here. They are, firstly, working from *the known to the unknown* and, secondly, working from *the concrete to the abstract*. A third is working from *the small scale to the large scale*. Lastly, a fourth characteristic is working from *descriptive definition towards explanation*. In planning a sequence of syllabuses in geography for a number of consecutive years, all these general approaches are adopted. On a smaller scale teachers will often plan learning of new terms, techniques and theories in exactly the same way. However, if these patterns of sequencing of work imply always starting simply, they do not imply that simple study (starting with the known, the small scale and the concrete) can be abandoned as pupils get older and more able.

Effective syllabus construction takes account of the fact that, as pupils mature, their levels of understanding develop. The point is made by several educationalists (for example, Bruner) that even as adults we often need to begin to learn very complex ideas by simple analogy (Bruner 1962). Bruner points out the need to spiral study so that pupils can return to studies in slightly more complex forms at subsequent stages, avoiding large intellectual jumps. These thoughts on syllabus construction owe much to work by psychologists on memory and learning. The suggestion of small step cumulative learning, featuring the need for frequent recall of recently learnt information, is sometimes referred to as programmed learning (Skinner 1953). Producing an effective syllabus for a year's course, or for a pupil's complete career in geographical studies in a school, involves teachers in planning exactly in this way. Preparing the right material for use in the right way at the best time is one of the exciting challenges of teaching.

A look at several types of syllabus, covering different approaches to geographical study, now follows. As a second set of illustrations, a brief look at aspects of the three Schools Council geography curriculum projects will follow in Part II of the book.

Examples of syllabuses

CONCEPTUAL STUDY OF SETTLEMENT FOR SIXTEEN- TO EIGHTEEN-YEAR-OLDS USING THEORY

If a whole school syllabus has been built conceptually, the pupils would probably have command of the basic terms, but of few stated theories by the age of fifteen. The syllabus illustrated briefly here starts from explanation rather than description alone, works at a larger scale in more abstract terms and with less familiar environments than studies for younger pupils might. Let us suppose that it is a study of varied aspects of *central place theory*.

Teachers might begin by suggesting that settlements influence one another and their surrounding land use in relation to their size, much as solid objects relate to one another under the influence of gravity. An analogue model could be introduced — that is, a model derived from parallels drawn from other subjects. A *gravity model* of this kind could be the starting point for looking at the friction of distance relationships between two settlements. Reference to map and quantitative data could be used to see if the model has relevance. A further stage would be, then, to suggest that for more than two settlements patterns are simply random, in reality, because of the complexity of variables in a normal landscape. By weighting size and distance, and plotting maps of central points within settlements, a *random model* could be tested, against the real distribution on a map, by using mathematical simulation techniques. Introducing specific theories of settlement patterns could follow. For example, the hexagonal lattice patterns suggested by Christaller based upon market, transport or administrative criteria could be introduced. Mapped areas studied at all stages could be from anywhere in the world — perhaps, but not necessarily, starting with British Isles materials.

A SYSTEMATIC SYLLABUS ON FLUVIAL LANDSCAPES FOR ELEVEN- TO SIXTEEN-YEAR-OLDS

Applying the principles of sequencing indicated above, perhaps a total five year sequence of work is worth sketching briefly here.

A modern syllabus covering this topic would require the availability of a rich variety of resources. It would be concerned with emphasising process, and would work within the framework of an equilibrium model, stressing that valley forms are the product, at any one time, of the balance of forces operating. In the first and second years of school, emphasis would probably be on learning definitions and explanations of terms which describe process as well as form.

One might expect the syllabus to start with work on the effect of rainfall on landform. Pupils could examine this either on the school playing fields, or by using a sand filled oblong tray and gently spraying water on to dry sand. Outside, in appropriate conditions, run-off, seepage into the ground and evaporation could all be observed. More easily perhaps, in a glass-sided sand tray, the level of saturated sand could be observed, and the idea of a watertable could be developed. Work both outside and on the sand tray could give opportunities for observing a distinction between sheet run-off and channelled flow.

Study of channelled flow would follow, developing again from outside work or cine-film. The use of the terms erosion, transportation and deposition, to describe the process carried out by flowing channelled water, could be learnt. The term watershed, defining the boundary of an area where all the surface water flows into one river system, could be introduced. By mapwork the beginning of a study of the patterns made by river networks could also start. Descriptive terms could be used for these according to shape – for example, radial, trellised and dendritic. It might also be appropriate, at this stage, to look at stream order from maps.

A sequence of work like this might be two years' contribution to work on fluvial landscape formation within a total geography course, which might, in the early stages, also include separately local studies and perhaps some work on the British Isles.

In the next three years a closer look at process would be in order. Because of the slow rate at which channelled water flow in rivers appears to affect landscape, or visually alters a river's course, sand stream table studies are often a good starting point. Controlled channel flow can exhibit, using irregular graded sand, most of the features of channel patterns and the process causes. Sand grains can be observed moving down channel, banks can be seen collapsing, sinuous courses developing, and braiding occurring. Similarly, deposition occurring on the inside of meanders from material brought down from the same side of the river, and meander belts migrating downstream can be seen. Delta formation can be seen, if the stream table is planned with a water body area at its low point. Other variables can be displayed. The visual observation and recording of the effect of process on form is something which field work cannot offer, unless pupils monitor the same stream, and measure and map features at regular intervals. This is, of course, an excellent idea, but more difficult for most schools than stream table studies.

From the process study, work could proceed on form from maps. For example, studies could be made of meander patterns to see if generalisations calculated on the relationship between meander length and meander width hold true. Studies could be made of historic and contemporary maps, which show that river courses have changed significantly in recent years. Well-known examples of map evidence include maps of the course of the Rio Grande, where it forms the border between the United States and Mexico. Meander cut-offs left United States territory on the other side of the river, after flooding. Subsequently the United States gave the territory formally to Mexico! As well as channel patterns, the long profiles of rivers would also form part of fluvial landscape studies, considering pool and riffle formation, for example.

None of this work as sequenced is outside the competence of the average eleven- to sixteen-year-old group, provided that terms are explained in simple language and that pupils observe and record evidence simply. This type of syllabus would form a firm foundation for raising much wider issues than the contribution of channel flow to valley formation. For example, the whole area of the mass wasting of valley sides has not been touched upon, and structural and lithological variables in the landforms largely ignored. The syllabus could be widened or lengthened as appropriate.

A REGIONAL SYLLABUS FOR THE SIXTH FORM

As an example of a sequence of sixth form regional study, examination of the European Economic Community will be taken. It will be viewed in terms of a systems model. The Community is, of course, not a closed system in the sense that life, livelihood, location patterns and processes within it are uninfluenced by outside factors. One need cite only the impact of oil price rises to make the point. However, a model which offers the opportunity to identify outside links in terms of inputs and outputs has advantages, when viewing an area which is not self-contained. It also has advantages in handling an examination of the Community internally as a whole, for it offers a model for presenting Community-wide structures and Community-wide interactions.

Use of this framework would lead to study of national state units only in subsystems terms, and only if they were relevant for specific purposes. No attempt would be made to work through a fixed set of topics — for example, on Eire or Denmark. Subsystems would be special purpose, perhaps single criterion regions. It would, for example, be useful to identify the main structural arteries which form the circuits along which people, goods, services and ideas flow. Several major axes stand out which would be masked by separate national studies. The Rhine valley region is a clear example. The English Channel is another. In industrial terms, the Birmingham–Ruhr axis functions as a subsystem. Dominantly agricultural areas can be seen as peripheral subsystems. Much more might be gained by examining the locational characteristics of the Scottish Highlands, upland Wales, Britanny and the Massif Central together, which have meaning in total Community terms, than ever could be gained by separate study. Focus on them, in this way, would help identify, classify and bring some order, and hopefully understanding. Regional synthesis has to be built out of an understanding of the functioning of the subsystems or boxes which help to build up total regional blocks. Many regional studies at sixth form level in the past simply described the separate content found in a subregional box. As far as showing interrelations were concerned, much regional geography did little to illuminate any appreciation of the synthetic nature of reality contained in regional landscapes. A subregional box remained an unilluminated black box. Systems theory can begin to help to make regions at least appear grey.

Present reality

Fifteen years after the first impact of the new geography in schools, none of the above illustrations of syllabus approaches and sequences should appear as a mere flight of fancy. True, perhaps only a minority of teachers is, as yet, consciously using a conceptual approach to content, but the number is growing. Further, more rigorously than before, teachers are using skill, knowledge and attitudinal objectives to plan effective learning. The examples above represent the styles of study that pupils, working with the new geographers, can and do experience. To present here a description of the study of river valleys within the evolutionary descriptive model known for sixty years in schools, or to present examples of how teachers use physically based regions in order to describe areas, would serve little purpose.

With this awareness of geography syllabuses, it will now be appropriate to turn to the issues raised by questioning the purpose of teaching geography.

5 Why learn geography?

Geography teachers have never been short of reasons why it is a good idea to learn geography. Listening to pupils' views on the purpose of studying geography makes it apparent that the beliefs in the value of geography as a school subject, which motivate some teachers, are by no means always matched by pupils' views. It would seem that an explicit clarification of aims can do nothing but bring teacher and pupil together. One of the significant trends in geography teaching has involved trying to do just this.

This is the result of a combination of factors, some relating to wider considerations of education as a process, and others relating to specific attempts to improve the quality of teaching. Both of these influences deserve general if brief consideration before looking at aims in teaching geography in particular.

Education as a process

The value an individual places on education may well be quite distinct from the value which society in general places on the outcome of that same education. A child may find learning about 'capes and bays' boring and valueless in school. He may just not want to know. Adult society, however, may be scandalised that pupils can no longer remember the names of capitals of countries. Apart from making news items perhaps less than meaningful, children might be barred from winning geographical quiz games for life! This rather trivial low-level example highlights the nature of the debate as to whether education is to be seen as something in its own right, as intrinsically worthwhile, or as something to be judged in extrinsic terms — that is, in terms of values which other people might place on the skills, knowledge or attitudes of an individual. The argument is well rehearsed in *Education as Initiation* (Peters 1963). In Peters's terms, education is seen as the development of the thinking being, not as the training of an individual in order that he might fit some external specification or role in society. Given initiation, the use a pupil makes of his education rests with him. Training implies restricted horizons which might prevent full development.

Improving the quality of education

Stemming in part from the idea that education has intrinsic merit, significant efforts have been made to try to identify the nature of the processes of education and find measures of their success. Both efforts focus on helping to make pupils aware of the intrinsic virtues of education. If pupils know what precisely they are doing, know how to do it, and can identify if they have succeeded, they are more likely to be satisfied and respond positively to future learning experiences. The geography lesson whose aim is 'to cover Africa in one period', backed by instruction to 'do your best to draw a map from the atlas putting on what you like', and finishing with 'it does not matter if you have not finished it, we will not need it again', is happily disappearing fast. The teacher had an intrinsic aim here, of a kind, but it was inadequately specified, made operational and assessed.

Teachers who specify extrinsic aims can present similarly ill-defined purposes. In the synopsis of a discussion by geography teachers, reported in *How Teachers Plan Their Courses* (Taylor 1970), the purpose of teaching about Europe is stated to be the fact that 'the children may visit there; they may also work in a factory which trades with Europe'. No useful educational course could derive solely from this starting point whatever the extrinsic truth of the matter.

Aims and objectives

Improvements in specifying educational aims really began as a result of the process of trying to break down general statements of purpose in such a way that they could be stated in terms of pupil activities and observed outcomes. This matter has already been raised at length in terms of trends in how geography is learnt, in chapter 2. It is worth simply reminding ourselves that general aims need breaking down into precisely attainable objectives, if successful teaching and learning are to take place.

Aims in learning geography

INTRINSIC AIMS

Of syllabuses examined from twenty-six schools in *How Teachers Plan Their Courses* (Taylor 1970) most syllabuses in geography spent most of their time setting out details of the geographical information which was to form the object of study. Information on method of teaching featured next. 93 per cent of the syllabus statements were concerned with content and method. Only 6 per cent of the statements were concerned with aims and only 1 per cent with assessment! It is evident from these examples that, at the time, the work of Bloom, or for that matter comparable work by Gagné (1965), as a means of helping teachers to spell out immediate intrinsic aims to assist lesson planning, had not spread very widely.

Such aims as are expressed tend to relate to the acquisition of skills which will enable pupils to differentiate and manipulate the geographical world around them while growing up. One recorded by Taylor was 'correct use of geographical tools, techniques and methods of recording information'. Another was 'to give a better understanding of basic terminology which will affect the pupil's daily life ...' A further one was to 'study the distribution of human and physical phenomena in the world, noticing how the two are related'. Some related to learning in general: 'to encourage individual research' and the 'production of neat work' are examples of this type (Taylor 1970). These aims relate to the contribution of geography to living a full and interesting life as a child. They are intended to arouse and resolve problems in pupils' minds, by stimulating and focusing curiosity. Twenty-three per cent of the syllabuses studied in *How Teachers Plan Their Courses* were identified as spelling out intrinsic aims. How the content, methods and concepts of geography may help promote intrinsic education is helpfully discussed by Bennetts (1973) in *New Directions in Geography Teaching*. In the broadest terms, the main intrinsic aim of all geography teachers must be to pursue the key intention of geographical study – that is, to enable pupils to handle, comprehend and be aware of the nature of location.

SOCIAL AIMS

Clearly one would expect that any subject taught formally, in an institution which brings children together for learning, would have social aims of a general character. The importance of behavioural attitudes has been touched on briefly before, yet statements of intrinsic social aims rarely feature explicitly in geography syllabuses. Rather, when stated, social aims relate to extrinsic and long term issues which some geographers feel they can identify as their concern. For example, the need for international understanding was noted in *New Thinking in School Geography* (D.E.S. 1972) as being used by some teachers to justify the teaching of geography in schools. The idea that 'the cinema, the press and most of all television have made available to everyone a general visual knowledge of the world', mentioned in the Plowden Report (D.E.S. 1967) is held by others to reflect a feature of contemporary society to which geography teachers in particular must respond. In more precise geographical terms 'to prepare a pupil for a place in society, by promoting a critical awareness of locational variables and society's impact on locational decision-making' might be a basic statement of social aims which would command wide support. Most syllabuses in the Taylor study, 52 per cent, emphasised social aims. Bennetts (1973) spells out in some detail the social aims often found in geography syllabuses.

UTILITARIAN AIMS

These extrinsic aims can be distinguished from social aims in that they stress more narrow concern with achieving publicly recognised standards of performance in examinations, and stress that the purpose of learning geography is to enable pupils to find interesting and secure employment after school. This definition separates them out clearly from intrinsic or social aims. From this viewpoint geography is seen in part as vocational training.

There was a stage when broad statements of the purpose of geography teaching had distinct imperial overtones. The control of an empire required the training of surveyors and cartographers. Many of them learnt their initial skills, and gained an interest in such employment, from geographical studies. The military and commercial connections of past empire and modern political and economic alliances involve businessmen and others in much more travel about the world. Courses have been taught in geography for commercial and bankers' classes in further education around 'what to wear, where'! Geography is taught specifically in military education establishments. There are Institute of Transport examination papers in geography. Perhaps the biggest single group of students, for whom the purposes of learning geography are stated in utilitarian terms, are those training to obtain employment in the planning departments of local government and the Department of Environment.

It is not altogether surprising that utilitarian aims become more explicit when geography is being learnt by older age groups. At this level, they are potentially meaningful and motivating. With younger pupils in schools, lessons or syllabuses tied to utilitarian aims would have little chance of success.

Why learn about location?

To justify aims by saying whether they are intrinsic or extrinsic and concerned with social or utilitarian values does not really answer the question 'Why?' Rather the justifications are concerned with how teachers propose to, and actually do, get pupils interested in the subject, or get them to opt to study in the first place.

There is limited evidence as to why actually pupils learn at all, and little or none on why they learn specifically about location. Theory would suggest that learning relates to the innate desire to seek the reduction of tension and stress, physical or mental, caused by the presentation of something previously unknown. Learning is really about basic survival and giving meaning to life. The theologians, philosophers and moralists may have an answer to the meaning of life. Interest in location may stem from one particular aspect of concern for survival.

PART II

Innovation in action

6 Project and school working together

An approach to geography teaching in the middle years 8–13, based on key concepts and objectives

Gordon Elliott, senior lecturer, Christ's College, Liverpool, and
Margaret Saunders, assistant teacher, Crewe Girls Grammar School

Local studies form the core of first year geography syllabuses in many secondary schools. An obvious advantage of this arrangement is that it enables pupils to do field work and use secondary sources such as maps. If there are limitations to such schemes it is that the local studies often become ends in themselves. In those cases where the locality is studied for its own sake, it is often left like a rudderless boat, floundering in the choppy wake of an expanding regional syllabus that rapidly moves on to studies of other areas of Britain and the world. Potentially fruitful links between studies of local and distant environments can thus be lost. This is a pity. There is much to be said for young children using experiences gained at first hand in the locality. They can be used to invest studies of distant environments with real meaning, and so rescue them from an empty verbalism that so often masquerades as teaching about other lands.

The scheme outlined here tries to tackle some of these difficulties, firstly by making what is learnt about the local environment as 'real' as possible, and secondly by linking it closely to studies of other areas of the globe. In this way we hope to break down the isolation of studies in the locality, thus allowing work on other environments to benefit from comparison/contrast with the local. It differs from most other geography schemes, however, by giving prominence to *objectives* and *key concepts*. By applying Bruner's idea that the foundations of any subject may be taught to anybody at any age in some form (Bruner 1962), we have tried to isolate some of the key ideas in geography. We then try to interpret them for young children, by adopting methods which maximise active pupil participation in the learning process, and at the same time help the development of learning skills by structuring them in an objectives based scheme.

The project in action

The work originated in October 1971 when Crewe Grammar School for Girls agreed to work with the Schools Council project based at Liverpool University (Elliott 1975). At that time the school's first year geography syllabus was organised in the following way:

1 Use of the sixteen points of the compass
2 Scale — meaning of the term and methods of showing it, e.g. linear, statement; draw plan of classroom to scale
3 Ordnance survey map symbols
4 Field work — simple exercise in neighbourhood
5 Cheshire — map to show neighbouring counties; relief and drainage map of county
6 A study of Crewe emphasising location and physical features, early railway history, industries
7 Cheshire — some important occupations, e.g. dairying, salt
8 Weather recording — knowledge of instruments; meaning of average rainfall and temperature
9 Latitude and longitude
10 Seasons, day and night

This represented a selection of topics that is fairly typical of such work in many schools. It was followed by studies of selected regions of the British Isles, and in the second year, of the southern continents. The situation was also representative in that some of the first year work was not taught by specialist geography teachers, nor were funds available for any radical approaches to new syllabus building, even if it had been desired. There were, moreover, the usual constraints of time allocation and the problems it brings. There was, however, a willingness by the geography staff to try out new ideas, and it was in this atmosphere of cooperation that the work described below was carried out.

In agreeing to cooperate with a Schools Council project, the geography department was making a conscious decision to open its doors to external influences that are not usually present in a school. Whether change was to be rapid or slow, however, or even to take place at all, would be the school's own decision. After all, the initial plans were that the project would be actively involved for four terms only, at the end of which it was up to the school staff to evaluate what had taken place, and make a professional decision as to whether any of the ideas were worth retaining. In adopting a partnership approach to curriculum development, we also agreed to share the labour of obtaining and producing materials for use in the classroom.

Project and school staff met on a number of occasions between October 1971 and Easter 1972 when work began in the school. The most significant meeting was a weekend conference in January 1972 when all schools participating in the scheme agreed to adopt the use of *objectives* and *key concepts* in their lesson planning (Blyth and others 1976).

Prior to this meeting the Liverpool team had constructed a set of *objectives* which emphasised the development of learning skills, as well as the fostering of certain interests, attitudes and values relevant to the study of Man in Time, Place and Society (Elliott 1975). For example, the use of skills in *finding* information and *communicating* findings to others were among those given emphasis. The idea was to give purpose, outside the intrinsic value of the chosen topic, to any studies undertaken by children. By pointing up objectives in this way, the project hoped that teachers would not neglect them or overemphasise some at the expense of others. Because we were concerned with a subject that had the study of Man in Place, Time and Society as its central aim, we also did not want to neglect *social* skills. To this end we set up objectives with the development of social skills as their purpose. For example pupils would be encouraged to develop social skills necessary to participate in cooperative projects. In particular we encouraged the development of *empathy,* the appreciation and understanding of others' behaviour.

The project was equally concerned to give careful consideration to *what to teach,* i.e. the selection of content, whether it be for an individual lesson, a topic lasting a month or the framework of themes forming the basis of a year's syllabus.

As professional geographers, many teachers have their own areas of interest and expertise. These contribute two important criteria in answering the question: What do we include in (or, more important, what do we leave out of) our lessons? But there are other important factors to consider when choosing topics for study. Relevance and a consideration of children's needs and interests are two which cannot be ignored. Moreover, the great changes which have taken place in academic geography in recent years make any consensus about what to teach increasingly difficult to achieve. So does the rate at which new knowledge is being fed into the teaching situation. It is often the impossibility of keeping abreast of new knowledge in a period of rapid change which has made teachers reluctant to change their own ways of teaching.

Work in school

To prevent this account from becoming too diffuse we have concentrated on the work done with first year pupils, although, as the diagram shows, we also applied some of our ideas to topics from the geography of the southern continents with second year pupils. The shaded parts of the diagram represent periods when the project was most closely involved with the school.

The ideas for study

The first term's work was designed around a study of *distributions* and *movement*. These two concepts were chosen because they are fundamental to a subject which is concerned with spatial arrangements. The frequent occurrence of indicator words such as *location, pattern, flow* and *migration* in geographical literature implies that an understanding of spatial distribution and movement is basic to geography. At the same time, it is apparent that these are very abstract concepts, and we saw it as a major part of our task to make them more meaningful to eleven-year-olds. We hoped actively

Project and school working together

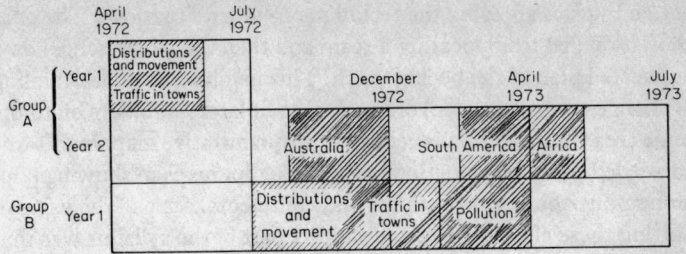

Figure 6.1

to involve the pupils in their study and, in this way, create a link between the existing syllabus and the new emphasis on concepts and objectives. For example, a study of scale and plan drawing featured in the school syllabus. We hoped to use both in a study of *location*.

In this context local material was to be used both as a vehicle for teaching skill objectives and as a contribution to a fuller understanding of the relevant concepts. This would then lead on to the study of similar phenomena on a national or world scale, giving a direct link between local and other environments, and at the same time enriching pupils' experience of the concepts being studied. So the initial scheme took on the following form:

Basic idea	*Scale*	*Skill/Activity*
Distributions	Locality	1 Describe your own location – use of landmarks
	↓	2 Use map to show your location
		3 Use reference system to show your location
		4 What is a pattern and how do we describe it?
	World	5 Locating features on maps by points

To give some idea of how we linked local studies with a consideration of other areas, it is worth looking at the scheme in a little more detail. The pupils used a duplicated plan of the classroom to show their own and other people's location on it. Once they had grasped the idea of people being represented by points there were many possibilities of applying the technique to other situations. The ones chosen ranged from locating a team and then the whole school on a duplicated plan of the hockey pitch. This involved an understanding of changes in scale (value) of the dots to fit larger numbers on to the same area — an idea that is central to all quantitative mapping. It was succeeded by an introduction to the use of dot maps in showing population distribution on national and continental scales. The value of putting these elements together in this part of the syllabus was that pupils had to grapple with problems of scale ranging from the local to global. At the same time they were being introduced to compiling maps of increasing abstraction. We reasoned that unless the most abstract maps (those on a world scale) were seen as part of an ascending order of things, some of which the pupils had seen and studied in their own locality, then the chances were that they would remain remote and abstract, difficult to comprehend, and would not convey the sort of messages their compilers intended.

This section of the work had dealt with people and objects *in situ*. Because many of the phenomena with which geographers deal are not static, and because geography deals with change through time, we felt it necessary to introduce some means of dealing with dynamic features. We started with movement around the school. In some ways this was an excellent choice. A lot of the problems studied by geographers are concerned with factors which channel and obstruct movement. These range from studies of channel characteristics in relation to river or glacier flow, to street/road patterns in relation to traffic flow.

In this work the pupils were actively involved from the start. It was framed around their own observations. After being taught techniques to illustrate these, they went on to consider their *own* solutions to some problems of movement. The basic principles of relating time/distance did not pose any real teaching problems, and the necessary working vocabulary of movement — peak flow, traffic jam, rush hour — emerged as a direct result of their studies of problems associated with movement around the school. We put this emphasis on the pupils deciding their *own* solutions to a particular problem because we hoped to develop *creative* responses to the

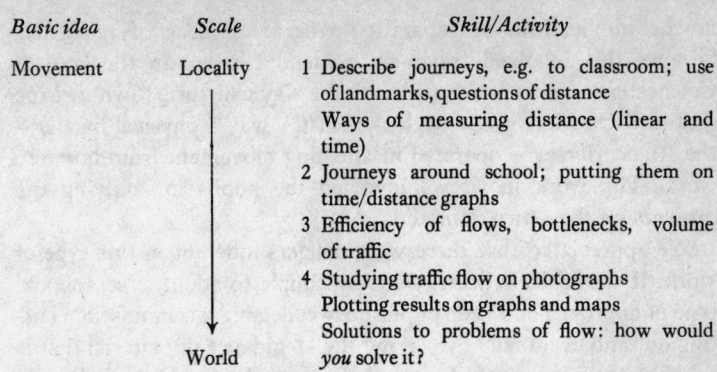

teaching material. Any 'there is only *one* right answer' mentality to this sort of problem solving would have been totally inappropriate. Many of the problems had several alternative solutions. All were viable. We were more concerned in encouraging the pupils to articulate their 'reasons why' rather than provide what they considered to be '*the* right answer'.

The ideas in action

In selecting a suitable topic to illustrate the application of these concepts in the real world, we chose traffic in towns. It could be studied locally, had relevance on the national and world scale, and there was a large amount of information available (much of it *free*). Inevitably, the vastness of the topic and the abundance of illustrative information posed problems of selection. 'What do we exclude?' became a real problem. This created an excellent opportunity for the use of the project's *key concepts* as aids in selecting what to teach under the umbrella of this topic (Elliott 1976).

On this occasion we chose *change* and *similarity/difference* as the *key concepts* and applied them through three case studies of traffic problems. These case studies differed in both kind and scale. They were of Crewe, Colchester and Merseyside. In each case, we looked at the implications of separating work and place of residence, because this involved travel on a massive scale. In the case of Colchester we were concerned with the way a historic town met the problem. On Merseyside we looked at the way a physical barrier – the River Mersey – operated in affecting movement from home to work. The work in Crewe involved the pupils in studying the problem on their own doorstep.

We appreciated that there were dangers inherent in this type of work. It would have been relatively simple to adopt a 'scrapbook' type of approach and keep pupils busy collecting, accumulating, cutting out and eventually displaying the abundance of material that is available on such topical themes. But to what end? As indicated earlier, the Liverpool project tried to link such studies to the development of skills. While there was plenty of opportunity for children to become interested in what the press had to say about traffic problems in general, our chief concern was to introduce pupils to some elements of geographical method used in analysing such problems. They were encouraged to look at the data selectively and critically, and formulate hypotheses about some of the problems – for example, people living the same distance from school should take the same time to get there. This led to the pupils being asked how they would account for differences in their own journey time, and how this might be changed by relocating the school. In fact, was there an optimum location for the school? As one pupil put it:

I think the best place for school would be where the houses are being cleared in Mill Street. Some of the advantages of having school here are, it is near the centre of where the people seem to live and there is a ready made space there. There are plenty of side roads off it where parents can park when they are taking and collecting people. There is a bus stop near, and also it is near town for when the school are going to the cinema or something similar. Some of the disadvantages are it can be quite a busy road and it also tends to be dirty from industrial places, the noise from the railway would probably disturb lessons. Also it would probably be quite dear to buy the land there and it would be hard to get across the road and out of junctions up town. I think the best thing to do would either be to have more than one school or leave it where it is.

By relating traffic problems to the pupils' own knowledge of traffic flows they were asked to design a traffic-free estate on the Radburn pattern. They were given a number of criteria on which to work – for example, 'people would want cars garaged as near their own houses as possible, but would not want their children exposed to the dangers of heavy traffic flows', and were then left to their own devices. In asking them which part of the year's work they had *enjoyed* most, this particular exercise was the most popular.

Basic idea	*Scale*	*Skill/Activity*
Accessibility	Locality	1 Pupils time journey to school and construct a time/distance map
		2 Relocating the school to optimum position
Change in urban form		3 Design own traffic-free estate
		4 Comparison of Crewe in 1880 with present to see how old urban form affects traffic flows
Similarity/ difference		5 Introduce ideas of traffic flow, census, peak flow
		6 How a river affects traffic flow – Merseyside
	World	7 How traffic flows in a historic town – Colchester

The work on Colchester was introduced by a set of eight slides showing some of the fine old buildings and streets in the town centre. The pupils were also given materials including a map showing the town in its regional setting, a copy of a sixteenth-century map of the town, colour pictures of attractive timbered buildings (e.g. the Siege House), a brief account of the town's development stressing its heritage of fine buildings, a modern street map showing the location of historic buildings and streets, a set of four thematic maps showing the town's importance as a shopping centre and place of work, with details of car ownership for 1965 and a projection of this map to 1981. There was some comparative material on other historic towns (e.g. Conway, Chester, Norwich) highlighting in general how the layout of ancient streets was totally unsuited to modern traffic conditions. The Bulletin of Environmental Education Study Sheet 1 provided useful illustrations of how the insensitive development of urban motorways can adversely affect residents. There was obviously a great variety of ways in which this material could have been used. One possibility was the provision of structured worksheets which would provide a guide through the material and an assessment of the pupils' understanding of the maps, pictures and statistics. As we had already used this method with similar material on Merseyside, we decided to adopt a more open-ended approach. As one of our objectives was empathy, as noted on p. 61, we decided to use a simulation to involve the pupils in the sort of decisions a committee might have to make as a result of the increasing volume of traffic in the town centre.

This would be a particularly thorny issue in a historic town involving many issues and representing many points of view. Do we knock down old buildings to make way for new roads? Do we pedestrianise the streets as an alternative? Pupils were asked to represent the views of various interested groups ranging from local shopkeepers whose trade might suffer to those interested in preserving the town's heritage. As a stimulus they were shown the film *Tide of Traffic* made for the Stockholm Conference on the Human Environment in 1971. What we were interested in was finding out whether the girls could and would enter into the spirit of the thing, selectively use the information they had been given, make out a case for their group, and then try to put themselves into the other person's shoes in the simulated meeting. We can quote one example:

I would like to address this meeting today as the spokesman for a number of business people in the area as well as on my own behalf. We all realise that there will have to be a solution to the problem of increasing traffic through the main shopping centre. Even so, the banning of cars from the High Street is affecting our trade and we feel that although we don't wish to lose our historic buildings some of these are almost beyond repair. One example is the Siege House which we all know is leaning. The demolition of the worst of these buildings and the building of a multi-storey car park would be a big asset. Pedestrian subways could also be built under the main streets without a lot of upset to private or business premises. We know this has already been done with success in the City of Chester with all its own historic buildings. Heavy traffic that is only passing through our city could by-pass it by the use of one of the main trunk roads.

Conclusion

It is evident that in participating in such activities the pupils were getting involved in the fascinating borderland between geography, politics, history, civics and planning. Whatever label we give this type of activity, it is evident that the pupils were being asked to develop a type of thinking involved in decision making, articulate their views in open discussion and, above all, involve themselves in the sort of issues many claim we ought to provide more room for in our geography teaching – those involving some discussion of values and beliefs.

7 Implementing a resource based project

Geography for the Young School Leaver

Alan Wheatley, head of resources, The Westwood High School, Leek, Staffordshire

Of nearly 100 curriculum development projects undertaken by Schools Council project teams, few have been as successful in the implementation of their aims as Geography for the Young School Leaver (G.Y.S.L.). Approximately one-third of all secondary schools in England and Wales are using the project's materials or ideas and, as was intended, curriculum development has occurred in many of these schools.

That G.Y.S.L. has given a considerable boost to the new geography, bringing it out of the university texts and into the classroom, underlies the fact that this project has not just produced a set of colourful teaching aids. The three kits (Man, Land and Leisure, Cities and People, and People, Place and Work) contain exemplar materials. The most important sections are the objectives which are clearly stated in the teachers' guide that forms part of each kit. These objectives are divided into *ideas, skills* and *values and attitudes,* as in the following example which comes from People, Place and Work, Unit 3, Part 1.

Ideas

* There are many different reasons for the decline of jobs in an area. These include:

   The exhaustion of physical resources

   The fall in demand for a product

   New techniques or equipment demanding fewer employees

   Forced movement of employment as site needed for other uses

High cost of production leading to closures
Closure of one part of an organisation as part of a rationalisation programme
Lack of money for investment
* The total unemployment and the rate of loss of jobs varies from one town, region or country to another

Skills
* Map, photo, text and statistical analysis
* Construction of simple statistical maps

Values and attitudes
* About the decline of employment in an area and the effects this has on the people involved

The introduction of G.Y.S.L. into a school must be done after due consideration of these objectives and the way in which they will affect the aims and objectives of the whole school curriculum and not only those of the geography, science or humanities departments. At The Westwood High School the introduction of G.Y.S.L. has thus been an important curriculum innovation and as such there are many aspects which have had to be considered.

The school

The school is a fully comprehensive, mixed, eleven- to eighteen-year-old age group of 1100 pupils. Geography (within the science area) is taught to all pupils from the first to the third year for one session of one hour and ten minutes each week. For the first year, the classes are in their mixed ability social groupings, but for the second and third year three broad ability bands are established.

Introducing G.Y.S.L.

We introduced the project to fourteen-year-old, average to less able, or poorly motivated pupils, for whom it was specifically designed. We feel that we require at least two years' experience working at the project objectives before we will be able to evaluate the situation and consider developing similar innovatory styles of learning and teaching with other age and ability geography groups. Clearly, the work has implications for all abilities in the fourteen- to sixteen-year-old age range and for both geography and interdisciplinary courses.

At Westwood, G.Y.S.L. has replaced the geography course usually followed by fourth year less able pupils. In recent years we have offered these pupils C.S.E. Mode III courses in local studies (geography and English), geography, and social history and geography (classical studies, history and geography). These courses were designed around basic concepts, further developing the skills, values and attitudes introduced in the first three years. The experience gained from developing these courses has been most valuable. It taught us that we could not introduce G.Y.S.L. without making some changes in the geography curriculum for the first three years. Very broadly, the course in the first year is locally based, while years two and three have a systematic approach to a general world geography. Thus, while the G.Y.S.L. ideas are new to the fourth year pupils, many of the skills are already developed, and values and attitudes have been discussed. This is important for it means that these pupils will have early success with their G.Y.S.L. studies, and this helps motivation.

Among the most frequent difficulties experienced in innovatory situations are: the size of the pupil group, the fourth year options system, the timetable restrictions, and the problem of getting adequate teaching space and adequate staffing with preparation time. At Westwood we have been fortunate in that the school is progressive in the way in which it has approached and accepted curriculum changes in all areas, and the tremendous depth and breadth of experience gathered, over ten years as a comprehensive school, was invaluable.

Public relations

Obviously, a head teacher and colleagues must be in sympathy with sound curriculum development or the barriers raised may render the innovation ineffective from the start. Colleagues should be prepared

Implementing a resource based project

to accept cuts in their capitation allowances to cover capital costs in the department introducing the new work. They may have to act as substitute teachers for geographers away on in-service courses. Therefore, colleagues have to be managed in such a way that they can have an overall view of the education of the pupils and appreciate the contribution the innovation will make. Geographers, of course, must be equally understanding.

Public relations is thus vital, and it is no accident that colleagues at Westwood have had the opportunity to observe G.Y.S.L. in action and to browse through materials in the kits. Parents have joined in mock lessons on open evenings.

Group size

In the first year of the innovation we had two groups of eighteen pupils. The size of the group has proved a maximum, because beyond this number techniques such as individual learning, visits out of school and role play exercises become unmanageable. However, to have a group very much smaller than this is not sound in staffing or economic terms in the present educational climate.

Fourth year options

It is worthwhile noting that there is a framework of options within which the fourth year pupils may choose to do geography or G.Y.S.L. Every pupil receives detailed individual help from his form teacher, head of year, the careers staff and subject staff, culminating in an interview attended by the pupil, his parents and staff. This ensures that the choices are made with a full understanding of the subjects involved, career prospects and pupil interest.

Timetable

Usually about 100 pupils will choose to take geography in the year and it is then the job of the head of department to establish sets based upon that number, the staff available and the ability and motivation of the pupils. A typical pattern would be:

One group of 34 – mixed G.C.E./C.S.E. Mode I
One group of 34 – C.S.E. Mode I
Two groups of 18 – G.Y.S.L. Group Mode III C.S.E.

Our first two groups were taught in parallel on the timetable, and the flexibility this gave us proved most important. Apart from being able to vary the group size, apply team teaching methods, show films together and have 'knowledgeable' cover in case of staff absence, perhaps the most beneficial aspect was having an instant support service in the room next door. If an idea is going well then it can be relayed immediately to the second member of staff. Should you have an 'off day' your colleague's enthusiasm is there to revitalise you. You can take it in turn to prepare material and visits for each other, exchange results or bring the two groups into competition on occasions. In our situation we found this complementary arrangement a great advantage.

The time allocation in the first year was a whole Tuesday afternoon (two sessions) and a session of one hour and ten minutes on a Thursday. Our thinking had been that the afternoon gave us the span of time required for local field studies and educational visits. It also provided for extended topic exercises where we could introduce a subject, work at it and have the conclusion drawn up by the end of the day. There can be no doubt that this arrangement was very satisfactory on these occasions, but on most Tuesdays our objectives were best achieved by methods which could be fitted into one session. The pupils were then faced with two consecutive sessions which, though related, were achieving different objectives and introducing new materials and skills. This often proved too much for them.

In the second year of the course, and for the new fourth years, we therefore decided to accept the disadvantage of two separate sessions each week. Where more time is required (e.g. studies out of school) we start during break and come back late for lunch, or allow pupils to go home from the place of study when they have finished at the end of the day, thus using the time usually taken to travel back to school. This does, of course, rely on the acceptance by the head teacher of such an arrangement and form teachers must be informed that the pupils will not be in for registration at the end of the day.

It seems to us that this attitude gives the pupils a degree of responsibility and privilege which helps in their eagerness to attain adult status. Indeed, the approach to these pupils is adult wherever possible, and there can be little doubt that they have responded favourably to this.

There are other changes and adaptations which might be necessary before G.Y.S.L. can be successfully introduced, or which may occur after introducing G.Y.S.L.

Cost

A prime consideration these days is expenditure. Few department heads find their capitation allowance sufficient to introduce all the innovations they would like. With G.Y.S.L. kits costing nearly £50 each it is usually going to be a case of approaching the head for special assistance beyond the normal annual sum. Under these circumstances, it is sensible to have sound arguments to put forward.

For instance, it is useful to borrow a kit for a short period, perhaps through an advisory officer or teachers' centre, and conduct some trials with pupils as well as public relations exercises amongst colleagues. At Westwood, the materials proved of interest to the English, humanities and general studies areas and subsequently they have made extensive use of them. While care must obviously be taken to avoid the possibility of pupils meeting the materials in two different contexts (though this can be advantageous in some instances), you nevertheless have a much stronger case for acquiring finance if you can show that it is a sound educational investment.

There are many instances of pairs and groups of schools sharing kits to save on costs, though it must be admitted that this does create many organisational problems because of the sequential structure of the G.Y.S.L. objectives. Perhaps a further relevant point is that, while units may be purchased separately from Nelsons, with care the materials should last for a number of years and the cost is therefore not recurrent annually.

Equipment

Other areas for consideration are audio-visual aids, and reprographic and library facilities. Each project kit contains a sound tape, 35 mm film strip or slides, overhead projector transparencies and master sheets, the latter intended to be copied by teachers for class sets. In the teachers' guide reference is made to 16 mm films, records, books and other sources which may be helpful for pupil use or lesson preparation. To take advantage of these materials and ideas it is necessary to have access to a range of hardware and other facilities. Owing to the structured nature of the course, it is wise to book such items well in advance to ensure the uninterrupted flow of lessons. At Westwood we have relied heavily on the availability of these items, and on video recording and playback facilities which allow us to use relevant television programmes.

While the project team has stated that it is in favour of emphasising the teacher's role in organising and ordering the learning experiences of pupils, as opposed to pupil-centred education, nevertheless the sensitivity to individual pupils' needs points clearly to the use of a wide range of teaching methods and therefore to the demand for equipment of all sorts. To achieve the smooth management and maintenance of this type of hardware becomes a prerequisite for this form of teaching and again indicates the value of a climate in which pupils will previously have had contact with, and learned to use, such equipment. As stated earlier, the kits contain exemplar materials and it is anticipated that teachers will want to adapt many of the items to local or more relevant examples. As there are also master sheets to be copied, the demand for reprographic equipment is going to increase. While line work can be adequately presented on spirit paper copiers, the use of photographs requires access to an electronic stencil cutter or offset litho machine. All this, plus the demand for visual and written material from libraries and numerous other sources, emphasises the very marked degree to which G.Y.S.L. forces the teacher to become an efficient manager of resources.

At Westwood we have been fortunate in having an established library resource service which coordinates audiovisual aids, reprographic and multi-media resources. Many departments are already experienced in this type of approach. In schools where this is not so, it is my experience that average and less able pupils, especially those with communication problems, do not get the full benefit of G.Y.S.L., certainly in the first few terms of the course.

Resources

In adapting G.Y.S.L. resources teachers will, of course, face the perennial problem of obtaining supplementary materials. Owing to the way in which G.Y.S.L. brings together many subthemes, the support material required, whether local or regional, will be scattered widely. It takes time to collect, collate and reproduce. Development of resource materials by teachers from groups of schools (as emphasised in Staffordshire) has helped solve the problem. G.Y.S.L. resources have been adapted and linked to local resources.

Units 1.1 and 1.2 of Man, Land and Leisure offer as resources pictures showing leisure activities. It is suggested that they might be categorised into individual, group, passive and active types. It is then suggested that pupils put their own activities into these groups, and locate the whereabouts and types of local provision, from the press. At Westwood, pupils start by completing a diary of a week's activities, and then look at 1.1 and 1.2 to discuss whether they think the pictures show what they regard as leisure activities, or not. Information is then collected on leisure activities for housewives, shift workers and old age pensioners. They are compared with pupil leisure pursuits. This minor example of usage makes the simple but important point that the published resources and suggestions for use are not intended as prepackaged complete lessons for instant use.

Project dissemination
The development of groups for discussion, curriculum development

and the production of local resource items has been central to the project's dissemination programme. Local education authorities were invited to send representatives to regional training courses. From the representatives a coordinator was appointed to act as a link between a group of schools in an area and the members of the project team. His job as link man was vital in the early stages, for the few project team members themselves could not assist all schools within any authority. Like most L.E.A.s, Staffordshire has held county meetings attended by geography and other interested teachers, the local team, representatives of the central project and the publishers, Nelson. The three teachers' guides were discussed, the experience of the project team and the teachers in the Staffordshire trial schools being the essential basis.

Most L.E.A. teams have carried out the type of work achieved in Staffordshire, those involved from the beginning being that much ahead. Initially our team spent considerable time in just exchanging teaching experience with G.Y.S.L., and helping each other with ideas for lessons and sources of materials. The coordinator attended the Mid-West regional meetings, held termly, and thus kept a close contact with the project team and other L.E.A. teams. Again, the motivation created through group work cannot be overemphasised and the regional meetings have thus been essential to the dissemination programme.

Having taught G.Y.S.L. for a while, the Staffordshire team has decided to concentrate its efforts in two main areas.

LOCAL GROUPS

Firstly, we have established a number of small working groups throughout the authority. Their primary function is to create local resources, the first county booklet having been published in 1975. However, there are many other developments occurring, such as the cross-fertilisation of ideas and techniques for other age and ability groups, the combining of schools for residential field studies, and an exchange system between schools to compare localities.

EXAMINATIONS

Secondly, the whole question of examinations was raised for discussion. Being in the early stages of introducing G.Y.S.L. into Staffordshire, the team felt that the safest starting point would be to write a C.S.E. Mode III examination syllabus (for awards up to and including grade one) around the G.Y.S.L. objectives, allowing for adaptations at a later stage and in the light of experience. A very brief summary of the assessment scheme is given below, as accepted by the West Midlands Examination Board.

Assessment scheme: marks out of 100

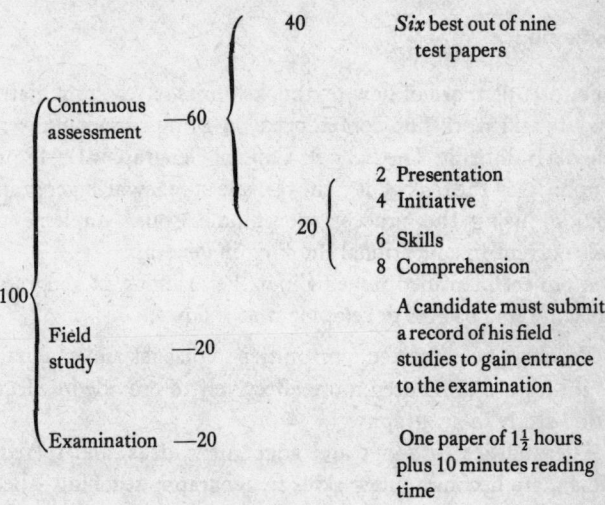

These two aspects of the work are very time consuming for team members. In the present educational climate everyone experiences difficulties in obtaining time for meetings and preparation of materials. It is a measure of the success of the G.Y.S.L. concept that throughout the country most teachers are somehow finding this time. The project is thus successfully achieving its long-term aim of curriculum development in geography.

8 Beyond the curriculum package

Teacher based curriculum renewal: implementation of the Schools Council Geography 14–18 project

Tony Gelsthorpe, head of the geography department, Fearnhill School, Letchworth, and project coordinator, Hertfordshire consortium

Introduction

In spite of a plethora of new textbooks, units of teaching materials, study kits and workshop conferences, on-going curriculum renewal in schools is difficult. The Schools Council Geography 14–18 project took upon itself the task of devising a cycle of renewal in geographical education, using the process, development and implementation models current in educational thinking in general.

The project identified issues about the teaching of geography in schools and its possible development as follows:

1 Teachers need more opportunities to discuss and evaluate new ideas if they are to be used more effectively to provide intellectually exacting study in geography.

2 The abilities to adopt and adapt new ideas, and to redesign curricula, are becoming new skills in geography teaching – because changes in the subject will continue.

3 Teacher based curriculum renewal is practical and rewarding when teachers have adequate incentive, support and feedback, and will influence the form, pace and assessment of their use of new ideas.

4 The extra work initially involved grows less as (a) resource oriented methods and reprographic facilities enable a reallocation of teaching time and resources, (b) new skills and roles are learnt.

5 The teacher based approach to curriculum renewal depends on

organisational support and flexibility, especially between schools and examination boards, which it is not possible for teachers themselves to bring about (Hickman, Reynolds and Tolley 1973).

In the light of its exploratory work, the project decided upon action in three major areas for its contribution to curriculum development. These were:

A supporting examination	*Work with schools*	*Supporting materials*
The devising of an examination to foster school based renewal	The clarification and promotion of skills in planning and evaluation in geography	Development of exemplar materials and strategies

Institutional and organisational support

THE SUPPORTING EXAMINATION

Much good work in curriculum development was seen to be going on in some schools, but because of the poor relationship between schools and examination boards and the impoverished nature of feedback this was not being recognised. There was thus a breakdown in what ought to have been a spiral of development, with curriculum renewal through innovative classroom strategies being adopted by the examination system, and rewarded in that system. Without such support and reward these developments were losing impetus. It was perhaps only in the extension of field work in schools, and its adoption for examination purposes, that any real progress was evident.

Thus an attempt was made to break the circle of underdevelopment by using the very institutional framework so often blamed for underdevelopment, the examination system. A linked system of internally assessed innovation and a common-core examination at G.C.E. O level were developed. A pilot project was undertaken under the University of Cambridge Local Examinations Syndicate in June 1974 (Reynolds and Stevens 1974).

The examination regulations illustrate the purpose of the examination and how this relates to curriculum renewal:

1 The purpose of this examination is to provide an assessment system which, while maintaining standards and comparability of assessment, encourages teachers to:
   (a) draw more effectively on new ideas in geography and education by the systematic and planned development of their individual resources in relation to changing curriculum needs
   (b) relate shorter-term subject objectives more effectively to wider, longer-term educational aims, particularly by giving more scope for individual study in depth, and constructive feedback to students
   (c) participate more fully in sustained processes of renewal at a time when the subject matter and potential strategies for geography teaching are changing rapidly

2 To meet these objectives, teachers are actively involved in the evaluation process, through the marking of course work and individual studies, and the submission of draft questions for the final common paper.

The system of examinations and assessment is, therefore, threefold:

Paper 1 Common final examination paper of two and a half hours (50 per cent of total marks), covering the core syllabus
Paper 2 Course work assessment (30 per cent of total marks)
Paper 3 Individual study (20 per cent of total marks)

CORE SYLLABUS

The framework for the core syllabus is illustrated in figure 8.1. Individual schools use this to plan their own curricula.

COURSE WORK

Figure 8.2 illustrates the relationship between the core syllabus, course work and individual studies. It also shows their complementary functions, allowing individual curricular planning and quick response to change in geography. The nature of the course work must ensure that pupils complete a total of six units of equal weight, representing two to four weeks study. The units cover regional or synoptic studies, planning problems, innovation studies and enquiry strategies.

A Illustrative examples to be chosen from	B Wider systems or contexts to be considered	C Appropriate distribution of examples chosen
(i) Weather and climate	Atmospheric and oceanic circulation	Local and British Isles 45%–65% approximately
(ii) Contrasting landforms	Long-term geologic and shorter-term geomorphic processes	Other developed regions of the world 10%–20% approximately
(iii) Conservation of natural resources	Hydrologic cycle	Less developed regions of the world 10%–20% approximately
(iv) Agricultural land-use	Physical ⎫	Wider physical and economic systems at a world scale 10%–15% approximately
(v) Location, growth and decline of industries	Technological ⎪ processes influencing spatial patterns and landscapes	
(vi) Transport networks	Economic ⎬	
(vii) Economic growth and trade	Social ⎪	
(viii) Settlement patterns between and within towns	Political ⎭	
(ix) Population growth and distribution		

Figure 8.1 The structure of the core syllabus (from University of Cambridge Local Examinations Syndicate, Schools Council 14–18 Geography Project)

INDIVIDUAL STUDIES

The final form of assessment used is based upon the results of indepth individual field study by pupils. The skills and concepts developed in the core syllabus and course work can be put into practice on a topic of particular individual interest. The organisation of individual work is of paramount importance. The development of such skills in the overall two year course is one which requires careful management in the total school context.

The studies are generally between 1500 and 2000 words long, but must not exceed 2500 words. They take the form of an argument related to a clearly defined question, hypothesis or problem. At a time when *all* field work might be suggested as, by definition, good geographical education, care needs to be taken to define the aims of the study. Successful field studies have shown (Chappallaz 1970, Gelsthorpe and Halsall 1975) and certainly individual studies undertaken within this examination should show evidence of an understanding of the use of sources and their limitation, the interpretation of data, the application of principles, the clarification of values, and the communication of the results of the enquiry.

Examples of individual studies proposed have included: 1 Do cliff profiles around Lulworth Cove vary with lithology? 2 How far is it possible to recognise distinct types of residential area in Letchworth? 3 What effect has containerisation had on the port of Felixstowe? 4 How well does the model proposed by von Thünen predict the pattern of land use around Ormskirk?

Implementation: the local consortium and dissemination

Groups of schools, with a teacher coordinator, seconded partly from full-time teaching, have worked cooperatively on problems of implementation, sharing experiences, resources and expertise. A group moderator, appointed by the examinations board, approves course design, offers support and advice, and sets the final common paper using teachers' draft questions.

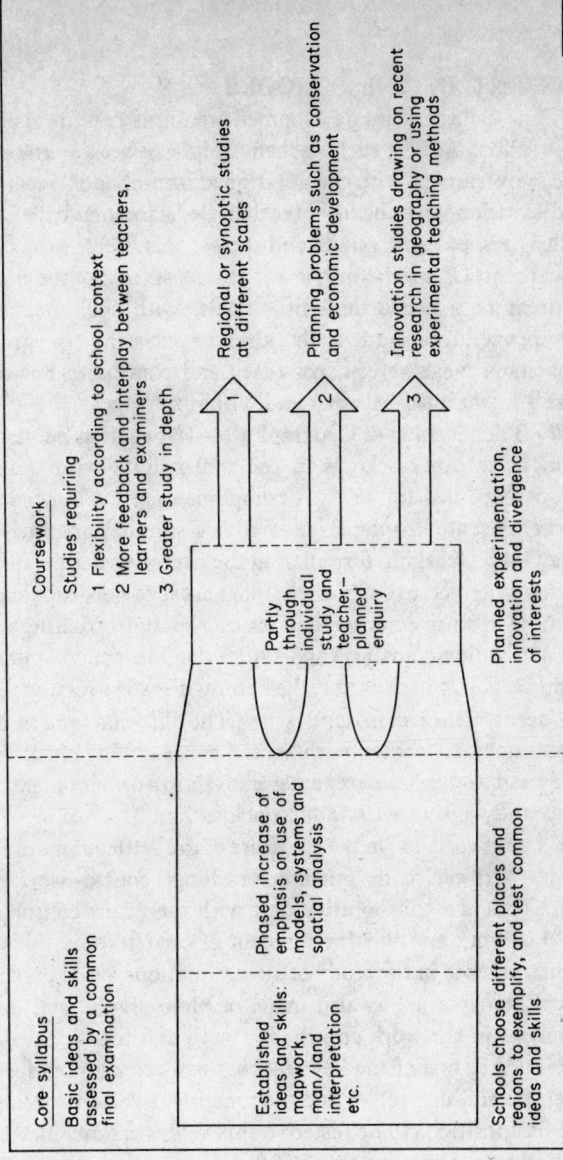

Figure 8.2 Core syllabus, coursework and individual studies (from University of Cambridge Local Examinations Syndicate, Schools Council 14–18 Geography Project)

MANAGEMENT IN THE SCHOOLS

The adoption of curriculum development requires careful management in the school. At best such a scheme might be seen as an operation in open government with consultation at a number of levels — for example, discussion with the head teacher, departmental colleagues, school colleagues, parents, pupils and the schools reprographic services department. Of special importance is the setting of the project in the context of a consortium of schools, with their particular timetable procedures and their already existing geography syllabuses. Some measure of consistency and continuity has to be achieved and maintained between and within schools.

Fearnhill The teaching of Geography 14–18 began in September 1975, as in three other schools in the consortium, with the first examination scheduled for 1977. A complimentary C.S.E. Mode III syllabus was presented to the East Anglian Examinations Board to parallel the O level work. In formulating the course structure all consortium schools agreed to cover three main areas of geographical investigation: man and environment issues, spatial structures and processes, and regional analysis and synthesis. The course units are shown in figure 8.3. It is clear that the natural disasters section of the first unit concentrates on man–land issues. The diffusion unit, by contrast, is essentially concerned with spatial process. The North East unit was devised to emphasise regional analysis in a development area through the study of themes in industrial location.

Figure 8.4 aims to show, in the structure of the settlement unit, the relationships between core syllabus teaching, course work and assessment. This is a collaborative unit with the whole consortium involved. Map work and the development of cartographic skills are the main instruments in the study of sites, situations and patterns of settlement. Extensive use is also made of photographs and quantitative analysis in the work on urban growth and functional zonation. Field study is one of the key teaching devices adopted for the study of settlement hierarchies and the function, size and spacing of settlement. Propositions to be tested in this field work include: 1 the larger settlements become, the wider will be their spheres of

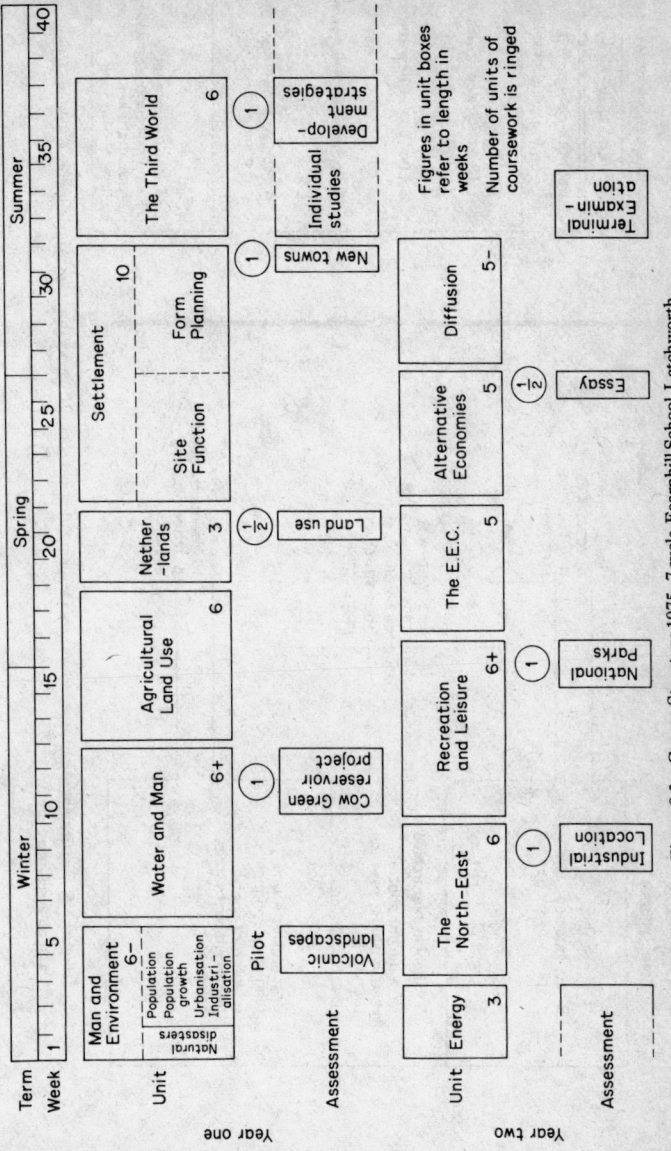

Figure 8.3 Course Structure 1975–7 cycle, Fearnhill School, Letchworth

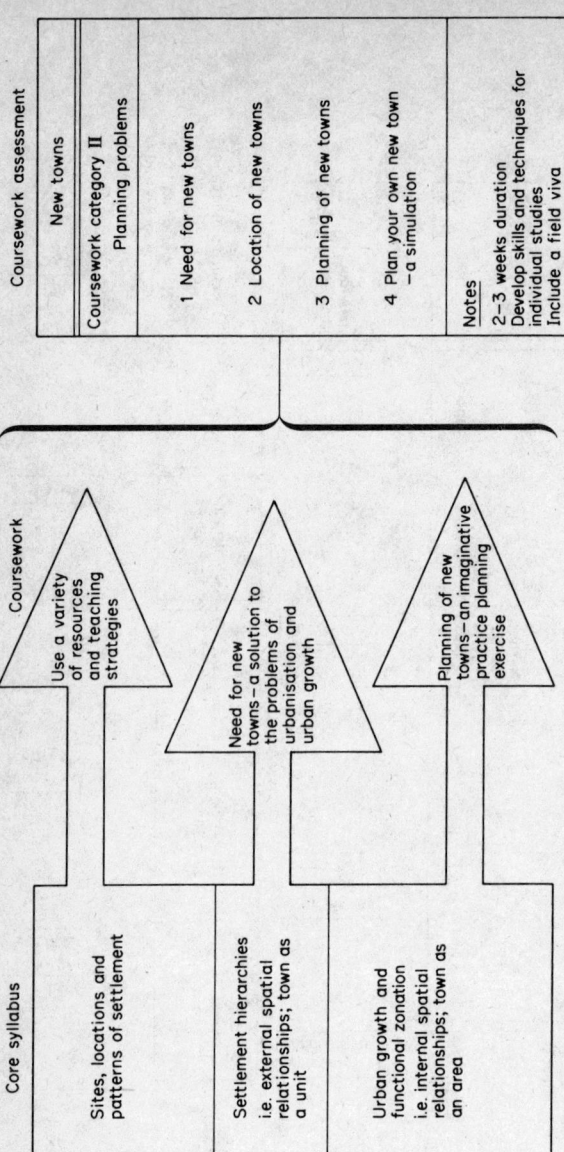

Figure 8.4 Settlement: A proposed structure (a teaching theme of about 10 weeks' duration to include core syllabus teaching and an assessment unit)

influence; 2 the larger settlements become, the wider the range of goods and services provided.

Work in this way on the unit makes it possible to emphasise the dynamic nature of settlements and the processes which sustain them.

ASSESSMENT

An attempt was made in the first course work unit to keep the structure and format on a comparatively traditional level. In the initial phase teachers and pupils felt greater security, and mutual confidence was established as a result. The unit included a simplified diagram of the landforms and geological structures associated with igneous activity. Questions tested generalisations about volcanic landforms related to type of eruption, erosion and the surface form of volcanoes. Landforms resulting from igneous activity were also considered. Assessment under time limit conditions is not necessarily most appropriate for course work. But in this assessment unit an attempt was made to go beyond traditional questions, to stress analysis and interpretation of diagrams and test the pupil's ability to sum evidence in support of generalisations. Contrasting styles of assessment are used on other units.

For example, the introductory resource material for the course work assessment unit on Water and Man is on the Cow Green reservoir project and outlines the conflict situation between the demand for water on Teesside and the provision of employment, with the great beauty and scientific interest of the site. Though a public inquiry was not actually held, the sources and documents available on the reservoir project (Smith 1975) offer an ideal opportunity for the formulation of a role play exercise along these lines. Organisation in the classroom involves individual pupils stating cases and presenting evidence from a brief to the public inquiry, under the chairmanship of the teacher. The roles include:

Against: A representative of Northumberland and Durham Naturalist Trust who is very concerned about the destruction of wild life. The Trust considers Upper Cow Green a better site.

For: An I.C.I. director who stresses the national benefit from an increase in the company's production. I.C.I. has a good reputation for scientific research and will give money for such research in the area of the reservoir before the dam is built.

Against: A tourist in the area at the time of the inquiry. He notes that the Pennine Way will have to be diverted and that water flow over River Tees falls could be reduced.

For: A trade unionist from Teesside concerned with unemployment. Dam construction and I.C.I. development are more important than preserving beauty.

Assessment is not undertaken at the inquiry. The chairman teacher summarises arguments and evidence in closing remarks. Pupils write assessments individually, state views for and against, and draw conclusions as to the consequences of any particular action.

Conclusion

It is hoped that this brief illustration shows that, through Geography 14–18, curriculum development and renewal on a permanent basis appears to be well under way.

9 A new examination syllabus
The Joint Matriculation Board A level Syllabus B

Ken Briggs, B. A., Canon Slade School, Bolton

A new syllabus in geography was introduced by the Joint Matriculation Board in 1975, and the first examination takes place in 1977. This new syllabus, referred to as Syllabus B, will for a time act as an alternative to the existing syllabus, Syllabus A, which was introduced in 1963.

The new syllabus

The construction of the new syllabus was begun in 1971. It was intended to take into account changes which have been taking place both in geography and in the techniques of examining, as well as changes in the J.M.B.'s O level syllabus.

Teachers in J.M.B. schools have been closely involved at all stages in the production of the syllabus. A draft syllabus was circulated to schools in the summer of 1973 and comments were invited. This syllabus comprised Paper I, concerned with physical geography, and Paper II, concerned with human geography, together with an outline of a scheme for testing competence in geographical skills and techniques by means of various kinds of practical work. An alternative to Paper II was concerned with the geography of the European Economic Community, but later this regional alternative was abandoned and it was decided that a complete new regional alternative syllabus should be produced.

In common with the trend in other J.M.B. A level subjects, the new syllabus is very much longer than the old, occupying five times the number of pages in the handbook (J.M.B. 1975). Details follow.

PAPER I: PHYSICAL GEOGRAPHY (THE NATURAL ENVIRONMENT)

Underlying themes are defined as (a) interrelationships between the component elements of the physical environment, and (b) the role of man as a factor influencing the physical environment and modifying natural ecosystems. The subject content is divided into four sections, comprising: (i) a background understanding of major land masses, types and categories of physiographic and structural units; (ii) chief types of landforms, their development and the processes at work under differing conditions of climate (including climatic change), lithology and geological structure; (iii) factors determining weather and climate, and the physical processes involved; (iv) characteristics of, distribution of, and factors in the formation of major types of soils and vegetation. Details of individual topics are listed in each of sections (ii) to (iv) and it is emphasised that stress should be placed upon interrelationships both within each section and between sections.

The detailed specifications of these sections suggest a marked change of emphasis compared with Syllabus A, and a considerably increased work load for A level candidates and sixth form teachers. Whereas Syllabus A specifies merely 'types of landforms', 'distributions' of climatic elements, 'characteristics and distribution' of major types of natural vegetation and simply 'an elementary knowledge' of soils, Syllabus B concentrates markedly upon 'processes', listing, for example, weathering, mass wasting, slope development, and fluvial, glacial, periglacial, fluvioglacial, aeolian and coastal processes in the 'landforms' section. The section on soils and vegetation contains reference to 'colloidal properties', 'ionic exchanges', 'soil catenas', 'plant communities, societies and associations' and 'vegetation climaxes and subclimaxes'. It is clear that the volume of knowledge of physical geography required of candidates has increased considerably, apart from the intellectual demands of comprehending quite complex interrelationships.

PAPER II: HUMAN GEOGRAPHY

The objective of this paper is stated to be 'to test the candidate's understanding of the spatial manifestations (patterns and processes) of human activities'. Six sections form the subject content: (i) population, (ii) rural and urban settlements, (iii) non-urban land use (e.g. farming and forestry), (iv) industry and industrialisation, (v) transport and trade, and (vi) regional interrelationships. As in Paper I, the emphasis in the new syllabus has swung away from descriptive geography towards 'processes'. Reference is made specifically to the Burgess, Hoyt, Christaller, von Thünen and Weber models, and also, less specifically, to 'interaction models' (Abler, Adams and Gould 1970, Haggett 1972). 'Commodities' have been discarded, and broadly replaced by references to 'types of rural economy and systems of agriculture' and their relationships to 'various levels of economic development', and 'factors influencing the location and development of extractive, primary processing, manufacturing and service industries'. Considerable stress is laid upon various aspects of locational analysis such as 'dispersed and nucleated settlement patterns', the 'nearest neighbour statistic' and 'nodes, links and connectivity matrices', together with associated concepts such as settlement hierarchies and interaction between and within regions. The trend is clearly away from the description of specific 'features' and towards the comprehension of 'universal' principles. The general aim of Paper II is to enable schools to inculcate in their sixth formers 'an understanding of how and why differences exist between different areas of the Earth ... through a knowledge of the spatial patterns of human activities' and 'an understanding of the concepts and general principles by which we seek to explain these patterns'. In the two written papers it is intended that 'knowledge of relevant information' and 'comprehension of concepts and ideas' shall be weighted in the ratio of 40:60. Compared with Syllabus A, there is no doubt that the amount of knowledge and comprehension of physical and human geography required of candidates has increased considerably; but this does not seem unreasonable since regional geography, which comprised almost half of the old examination, does not appear as a specific requirement in the new syllabus. Teachers are advised, however, that their candidates should be able to illustrate their understanding of principles and concepts by reference to 'selected case studies' at various scales ranging from the global to the local. This gives teachers a very welcome degree of freedom of choice in the development of their courses, and guarantees that examination questions will not be focused directly upon specific, named areas. Candidates will be able to use in their answers any relevant regional knowledge which they may possess.

PRACTICAL GEOGRAPHY

The third part of the syllabus is intended to encourage sixth formers to acquire 'an understanding of, and competence in, a variety of skills and techniques by which geographical data may be obtained, analysed and presented'. Skills and techniques specified in the syllabus are those relating to (i) the use of topographical, geological, soil, land use and weather maps, (ii) the study of air photographs, (iii) field work in both physical and human geography, (iv) the statistical analysis of data, and (v) the cartographical presentation of data.

Candidates may choose to have their competence in these skills and techniques assessed either (i) internally by the teacher on the basis of either three small-scale (1000–2000 words) practical projects or one large-scale (up to 4000 words) project carried out during their A level course, or (ii) externally by means of a practical examination of $2\frac{1}{2}$ hours. The Subject Committee has expressed its preference that the internal assessment alternative should be regarded as normal, and that the practical examination should be taken by only a minority of candidates.

A booklet of extremely helpful notes for the guidance of teachers in organising, supervising and assessing the practical projects carried out by their students has been published and circulated by the Board (J.M.B. 1974). In this booklet a list is given of titles of projects which have already been carried out in schools in South Yorkshire and North West England. The following selection of titles suggests some of the possibilities in field work and non-field work studies in physical and human geography at a variety of scales: (i) 'An investigation of the development of drainage patterns on a spoil heap at Denaby, South Yorkshire', (ii) 'Moisture surpluses and deficits in South America, using Thornthwaite's techniques', (iii) 'Land reclamation in the North Yorkshire Moors', (iv) 'The effects of motorways in improving accessibility to London', (v) 'The growth of the Bradshaw area since 1845: a Monte Carlo simulation'.

This section of the syllabus adds still further to the freedom of choice which is made available to the teacher. He is enabled to focus his teaching of geographical skills and techniques upon a programme of creative research work among his A level students, based upon projects of a size and scale best suited to their abilities and aptitudes. The dangers of the over-use of local field work resources, and the duplication of field work projects in schools with large sixth forms, are avoided by the introduction of the possibility of basing projects upon data other than those collected in the field. In addition, the teacher is able to use his personal knowledge of his pupils in the assessment procedure. Their 'quality' is no longer determined by a complete stranger after six hours of isolation in an examination hall. This represents a substantial devolution of power away from what is sometimes regarded as the impersonal bureaucracy of the examining board. The opportunity is provided for the development of a new spirit of cooperation between teachers and examiners.

The new assessment procedures

Two written papers (Papers I and II) will be taken by all candidates. Each of these will have two sections (Sections A and B). Section A in each paper will contain eight essay questions, of which candidates will be required to answer two. Section B in each paper will contain six data-response questions, of which candidates will be required to answer two. Normally, therefore, a candidate's performance in A level is to be determined on the basis of (i) four essay questions, (ii) four data-response questions, and (iii) either one large-scale or three small-scale individual projects.

THE ESSAY QUESTIONS

Essay questions of more or less the traditional style have an important, though not a dominant, place in the new examination. It appears that most teachers and examiners believe that the ability to write an extended essay on a given topic is an important indicator of a sixth former's geographical ability. The essay is regarded as being capable of testing a candidate's ability to be critical, to select information from his memory, and to use it in such a way as to convey a clear, structured argument to the examiner. Hence, in this examination, 40 per cent of the marks are to be allocated to essay questions.

It may well be, however, that the freely written essay suffers from certain disadvantages as a mode of assessing ability in geography. It may tend to give an 'unfair' advantage to highly literate candidates who possess good memories, and may also tend to encourage teachers to place excessive emphasis in their teaching on the supply of verbal information to their students. Also, there are certain problems in the standardisation of the assessment of essay answers by large numbers of examiners, who may tend to differ in their judgement of quality and relevance.

The reduced weighting of the essay component in the new examination is a reasonable compromise, and seems likely to give greater opportunities of success to a wider range of candidates displaying a broader spectrum of geographical abilities. Careful phrasing of essay questions and an emphasis upon the theme of interrelationships should be capable of reducing the difficulties outlined above to manageable proportions.

THE DATA-RESPONSE QUESTIONS

The introduction of data-response questions to replace some essay questions seems entirely praiseworthy. In this type of question, the candidate is presented with information in the form of maps, diagrams, photographs, statistics, etc., and he is required to answer a small group of questions which relate directly to this information. The examiner is therefore able to set questions which do not depend upon the possession of a particular body of knowledge, but which may be capable of testing the higher cognitive abilities. A candidate may, for example, be provided with a land use map of a town with which he is unfamiliar, and he may be asked to explain the pattern of land use. In answering this question, the candidate is compelled to exercise his comprehension of various geographical concepts which he has acquired during his course, and to apply this comprehension in an unfamiliar setting. Comprehension therefore is of much greater significance than the ability to recall factual information.

Teachers confronted with the task of preparing candidates to answer this type of question are likely to conclude that much of the traditional, essay oriented, information based style of teaching is somewhat irrelevant, and they may feel obliged to develop more flexible programmes of pupil activity, based upon the solving of problems and the analysis of data. Such questions are also likely to assist in the assessment process. Standardisation of marking between examiners is likely to be facilitated, since each candidate is supplied with exactly the same amount of information. Hence, assessment can be based purely upon the candidate's interpretation of the data.

A problem associated with this type of question is that in each paper the candidate has to make a choice of two data-response questions from six. Unless the quantity of data included in each question is relatively small, this selection process may take some little time. Candidates in fact are to be advised to spend ten to fifteen minutes in selecting their questions. There seems little reason why candidates should not be encouraged in this way to plan constructively the use of their time in the examination room. The new examination makes it quite clear that it is not a good policy to write furiously (and possibly repetitively) throughout a whole examination.

Considerable support has been indicated by teachers for the introduction of objective testing into the assessment process. In an objective test the candidate is presented with a large number (up to fifty) of short questions, some of which may be of the data-response type. In each question the correct answer is selected from a number of alternatives (usually five) which are labelled A, B, C, D and E. This style of testing has two main advantages. In the first place, questions can be designed in such a way as to test particular specified abilities, with a minimal amount of 'interference' from the candidate's skill in literacy. In addition, marking is completely objective in the sense that it requires no knowledge or judgement at all. In fact, such tests are commonly marked extremely rapidly by machine. This type of assessment will not be used in the first place, but may be considered at some future time.

THE INTERNAL ASSESSMENT OF PRACTICAL GEOGRAPHY

The arrangement is to be that the teacher assesses the performance of each of his candidates in respect of the collection, organisation and interpretation of data by awarding a mark up to a maximum of 20, this total accounting for 20 per cent of the marks of the whole examination. Useful descriptions to guide the teacher in placing his candidates in various mark ranges are supplied by the Board (J.M.B. 1974). Projects will not be re-marked by external examiners, but a statistical moderating procedure will be applied by the Board. In his assessment of his candidates' performance in practical geography, the teacher will tend to be evaluating abilities which may not become evident in the written papers. Here, of course, the ability to recall information is of little importance. The teacher may look for qualities such as initiative and perseverance in observation or the collection and recording of data, and skills in the fields of graphicacy and numeracy in cartographic representation and statistical manipulation of data respectively. He may also assess the candidate's ability to interpret his data and to evaluate the success or otherwise of his investigation.

Conclusion

The new syllabus seems likely to have a wholly beneficial influence upon the quality of geography teaching in J.M.B. schools. Teachers are clearly encouraged to develop courses which successfully integrate (i) the acquisition of knowledge, (ii) the comprehension and application of principles and concepts both theoretically and in relation to practical investigations, and (iii) the development and practice of graphical and numerate skills. This represents a much broader range of objectives than could ever relate to a simple essay type examination. Assessment procedures are shared between the teacher and the Board, and are concerned with an extremely wide range of geographical abilities and skills.

The new syllabus should not be regarded as an attempt by university academics to impose their ideas on modern geography upon subservient schools. Practising teachers are strongly represented on both the Subject Committee and the group of examiners which is responsible for organising the examination. The response by teachers to the draft syllabus circulated in 1973 was overwhelmingly favourable. It would be more correct to regard the syllabus as a statement of what teachers would like sixth form geography to be.

10 A school based development

Cities of the United States: an urban geography work unit for third years

David Jones, head of social science faculty, Northicote High School, Wolverhampton

This work unit, which has been in use in various forms for four years, was developed as a response to several stimuli. First, the third year scheme is concerned with the theme of contrasts of wealth and poverty, and Cities of the U.S.A. was written as an example of urban geography in a developed country, its partner being a unit on urban geography in Latin America. Second, although examples of cities could have been taken from anywhere in the world, the unit originated at a time when an abundance of new audio-visual material became available in the form of B.B.C. radio and television series. Third, a work unit based on the understanding of concepts, rather than the learning of a body of facts, was necessary to continue the concept oriented work done by pupils up to this stage. Fourth, an essentially resource based unit was felt to be appropriate for the needs of teaching mixed ability groups, with individual work rather than class work forming the core of the unit.

The end result was the production of a kit of materials which included textbooks, pamphlets, maps, video tapes, audio tapes, film strips and slides and the worksheets which were the pupils' guides to the work they had to do. To accompany the kit a 'concepts' sheet was written for staff. The notes added to that sheet give some idea of the thinking behind the unit:

The work is based on ideas not on description. Most of the ideas are made explicit, but not necessarily using the words used here. Discussion with individuals and small groups is essential. Class lessons are rarely appropriate and work should progress individually.

Few pupils will complete all the work available. Use your own judgement to decide which parts of the work a particular pupil should omit. Where necessary develop additional exercises to slot into this scheme to consolidate particular ideas.

Originally the work unit was closely based on the radio and television programmes because they provided such good material. Even when it was first used, however, the unit could be followed without these particular resources, despite their great value.

It would give the wrong impression of the way the unit was developed to claim that it was done in a textbook fashion, with the course objectives being specified first and then the materials and exercises assembled to meet them. It was done in a far more empirical way. There was a mass of superb resources which were approached from the point of view of the ideas they could teach about urban geography. There were many ideas which could have been taken up on the worksheets but were ignored, either because they were of marginal importance or, more often, because there was not the time to use all the material to the full. Very often these were brought up in individual discussions. The ideas with which the worksheets were concerned were summarised on the 'concepts' sheet, the term concept being used in its widest sense. This extract from the 'concepts' sheet relates to the work on New York, and it should be noted that it is a guide to teachers, not a list of words for pupils to know.

New York: concepts

1 Urbanisation
2 Site
3 Location
4 Agglomeration
5 Functional zones
6 Dispersion
7 Gradient
8 Rent

9 Income/residential area relationships
10 Morphology
11 Urban problems

On a broader scale, the work unit was taken as the basis for comparison and contrast with the Latin American cities unit which was studied later. In both units, U.S.A. and Latin America, the work was concerned almost entirely with the internal structure and processes of cities.

The work unit began with an introduction which dealt with the degree of urbanisation in the U.S.A., which was then followed by the core of the unit, the work on New York. This was followed by Laramie, a seemingly strange choice, but the radio programme was so good, and it illustrated so many points at a completely different scale, that it would have been a waste not to have used it. Dallas and Detroit were the two cities on which most of the other work was based, but additional material was prepared on Chicago, Boston, San Francisco and several other cities, these often being short exercises based on limited amounts of data. The whole unit concluded with an exercise on the pattern formed by the major cities of the country, so that pupils were able to locate the cities they had been studying.

The large number of sources of information, the wide ability range of the classes and the varying work speeds of individuals meant that there had to be some means of telling pupils where to find particular bits of information. Rather than include the sources on the worksheets a chart with all the alternative sources was produced, often giving pupils a choice of different books and sometimes different media.

The worksheets all followed the same pattern of having a series of questions linked by a text which sometimes gave the answer to the next question or gave a lead which had to be followed up elsewhere. This extract from the worksheets, the New York work, was expected to be completed by all pupils, and despite the apparently difficult nature of some of it, was finished by all except the most chronic absentees. Most pupils, in fact, went well beyond this in the five to six weeks allowed for the unit.

New York

We start with a problem. What is the population of New York? If you look it up you will probably find several answers. You first have to decide what you mean by New York. The population of the whole built-up area is over 16 million, the population of New York City is about 8 million, while another figure you might find would say nearly 15 million. This is for New York City plus the built-up area immediately around it. The map on the separate sheet shows these different areas.

1 Write a few lines about New York's population.
2 Draw a map to show how New York has spread out into three states.

The site and position of New York

New York began as a small settlement on Manhattan Island.

3 Study the maps and photographs and explain the advantages of this site for a city which became one of the world's major ports.
4 Draw a map to show New York's position in the North East of the U.S.A.

Manhattan

The road pattern on Manhattan Island is typical of many cities in the U.S.A. It is called a 'grid iron' pattern.

5 Explain why the road pattern is given this name, then explain the naming and numbering of the streets.
6 On a map of Manhattan mark the two areas of skyscrapers for which this part of New York is well known. What are these areas called? How do they differ from each other?
7 Explain fully why there is so much office space in Manhattan. Say why the land is so expensive and why buildings in the business areas are so tall.

Some people are becoming worried that Manhattan might lose its importance as a business centre and that companies will move their offices elsewhere despite the advantages of the place.

8 Make a list of the disadvantages of Manhattan from the point of view of an office worker.
9 Name one company which has moved its head office from Manhattan. Where have they built their new offices? What are the advantages of the new location?

As well as providing jobs in offices, Manhattan is a manufacturing area. Lower West Side (between Midtown and Downtown) is important for making women's clothing as well as for specialized types of printing.

10. On your map of Manhattan shade the industrial area just mentioned. Do not use the same colour you used in your answer to Q.6.

You are now beginning to build up a map showing the different land use zones of Manhattan.

11. Using different colours again, shade in and name the one large area of open space on the island. Much of the rest is housing; shade it using another colour. Name the area called Harlem. Give your map a key.
12. How does Harlem differ from Midtown and Downtown Manhattan?
13. Why is it that many of the people who live here in the centre of New York are the poorest people in the city?
14. Why is the city government short of money? What effect does this have?
15. All big cities attract immigrants from other areas, whether they come from other parts of the same country or from another country. Who are the most recent immigrants to New York? Where have they come from? What problems do they face?

The spread of New York

You have already drawn a map to show how New York has spread out into three states (Q.2). On the map which shows New York's population the central part is losing people while the outer parts are gaining people rapidly.

16. Write down as many differences as you can between people's homes in central New York and in the outer parts of the built-up area.
17. Draw two squares with 2 inch sides. One of them represents a patch of land in Harlem and the other a patch of land on the very edge of the built-up area of New York. In one of the squares put five dots to represent the five people who live there. In the other square put 120 dots to represent the 120 people who live there. Label the two squares to show which is Harlem and which is on the edge of the built-up area. Each square represents one acre of land.

The way New York is spreading is typical of most large cities in the U.S.A. If it continues to grow and if the other large cities on the Atlantic coast continue to grow there will eventually be one large city stretching from Boston to Washington. This new city has already been given a name, Megalopolis.

18 Name the cities which will be part of Megalopolis. For how many miles would it stretch along the Atlantic coast? Draw a sketch map to show its spread.

During the course of this work on New York pupils looked at the television programme. Ideally they would have seen it in small groups at the most appropriate time but this was not normally a practical proposition, in which case the whole class viewed the programme together. Where a film strip or slide was needed the equipment was used by individuals or small groups as and when it was required. In most cases there was also a home produced tape commentary to go with the film strip and duplicated notes to go with single slides. To avoid moving equipment to several different rooms, the rear of the main geography room was set up as a small studio where these groups could work independently for short periods. This resulted in surprisingly few behaviour problems.

The individual nature of the work, the provision of varied resources and guides to these resources did not lessen the teachers' classroom activity but left them free for the crucial task of discussing the work with individuals and small groups. This was essential for two reasons. First, to ensure that pupils understood the ideas in the work and to take them beyond the immediate tasks by extending them with probing questions, or, where necessary, to provide alternative material where difficulties were found. Second, to ensure that everyone was really working hard, and that the boy or girl 'sitting thinking' really was doing that and not sleeping for the whole lesson.

Where a multitude of resources is used home work can be a problem. Most of the materials were in demand by several classes at once, there were limited stocks of some of them, and to check them in and out each lesson would have been virtually impossible without devoting too much time to the task. The problem was overcome by setting a series of separate, parallel exercises which either tested work already done in class, or examined some related topic not dealt with in the main class work. For example, one such exercise dealt with the importance of the ten largest cities of the country, while another examined the importance of the car in American life.

Assessment of pupils' understanding of the ideas contained in the unit was necessary from the start. To a considerable extent the unit was self-testing since later sections demanded understanding of earlier work, so in the short term progress or lack of progress could be assessed quite quickly. In the longer term, assessment was not initially very satisfactory due to the difficulties encountered in writing good examination questions. The temptation to ask questions which were easy to write but demanded only definitions or descriptions was very great. The most satisfactory type of question involved the application of the ideas of the unit to new problem situations using data which were fresh to the pupils and demanding little if any factual recall.

During the period of its use the work unit has been rewritten three times to place less reliance on the B.B.C. material and to take advantage of newer materials, but it is still basically the same as the original which has been described here. It appears to be a successful blend of information on factual situations and ideas, and the changes have been only in the resources used and the wording of questions. The thinking behind the unit is unchanged, with the emphasis still strongly on the understanding of concepts concerning cities which can be applied in many situations and not on the description of particular cities.

PART III

Future change

11 The knowledge explosion

The present situation in schools still includes some geography teachers and their pupils who are attempting to find meaning in locational studies by using the data collection, processing and evaluation methods of the explorers of the nineteenth century. Pupils leave school having learnt to classify, map static features and ponder, but little else. The present situation also includes, in increasing numbers, teachers and pupils who use scientific methods characteristic of the natural and social sciences in the twentieth century. Pupils leave school having learnt to evaluate theory, comprehend static and dynamic representations of space and articulate points of view about known problems. We can confidently expect the nineteenth century model to disappear. It is not necessarily clear, however, that the model this century has offered can be predicted, with any confidence, as being able to handle the future.

We can usefully start a consideration of the future by asking a question echoing the question in chapter 1. What is the content of geography likely to be in the rest of this century? Such a question has obvious dangers. Change appears unpredictable in so many respects. Yet surely the question must be asked; if it were not, and had not been in the past, geographical study might still simply be concerned with passing on classical views of the world as divided into temperate, torrid and frigid zones.

Location would seem to me to remain the central focus of study for geographers. The future will probably not involve the need to redefine geographical study, but it does hold the problem created by man's vastly increasing knowledge of location. At all scales more data, in more varied and complex form, are now potentially available for use.

The local scale

At local study scale in schools, published maps need not be relied upon as the basic form of representation of spatial data, and increasingly they should not be relied upon to give accurate representations of contemporary distributions or patterns. For the processes of cartographical transcription cannot cope with the effects of the speed of change at the moment. If school pupils are to handle reasonably contemporary data, and not become historical geographers, they must use in locational studies the most recent knowledge that is available. In spatial structural terms, this means turning increasingly to the use of mosaics of vertical air photographs. For planning purposes, local government holds photographic cover of its area, and cover is held nationally at scales which pupils could use. The greater regional detail available on photographs needs bringing into the classroom.

Again at local government and national level, vast amounts of data are banked in computers. Much has locational significance. The Department of Environment uses computer models to simulate present and future traffic flows, for example. We shall probably have to accept a time lag in publication as inevitable. The real problem is that data are collected, and controlled largely by non-geographers, at the behest of others, certainly outside the schools. Lack of access to knowledge and control of knowledge represent the real barriers. Educational use of data has a fairly low priority in our society. Geographers will need to make advances in gaining access to data, as well as in handling them, if they are to make a continuing contribution to aiding a pupil's understanding of the real world. It will need the concerted efforts of academic geographers and teachers both in this country and elsewhere.

The international scale

On the global scale also, vast amounts of locational information are stored away, in visual and computer form, which have not yet seen educational daylight. Earth resources satellites transmit pictures back to receiving stations in black and white, true colour, infra red and a variety of other forms. Sensors on satellites gather quantitative measures of the environment. Military surveillance satellites collect information on locations as small as 6 inches in size. Continuous global orbiting means that changing locational problems can be recorded daily, weekly or monthly. Spatial change and process have been and will increasingly be recorded. While some information is deliberately made available and continuously updated because of its global impact, many data remain firmly locked away for 'security' reasons by national governments. One of the few areas in which data have been made available globally from satellite sources relates to the weather. Vastly greater understanding of the three-dimensional interacting nature of the atmosphere has resulted. Advances could not have been made without these data. For example, in schools, meaningful knowledge of the winds in the upper atmosphere, particularly the mid-latitude jet streams, did not exist fifteen years ago. Explanation of surface air movement has been transformed as a result, and the mysteries of the mechanics of depressions and their tracking paths made clearer.

Study of data from the historic past, which can mean ten years ago given the increasing pace of change, could have increasingly damaging effects on geographical study in schools. If there is a factual gap between knowledge in use in schools and contemporary fact, this needs to be known. Refinements in methods of learning will be of little avail if the locational data are incorrect.

The way ahead

The first task of academic and school geographers for the foreseeable future is to gain access to the knowledge explosion about location, so that they can continue to offer it order and meaning. Teachers must become personally resource hungry, and not await the appearance of textbooks and resource kits. At a national and regional scale, I would argue that there is hope that a barrage of requests would not go unheeded. But perhaps there is also scope for bodies such as the Geographical Association to attempt to obtain information and offer a data bank service with on-line access by schools. It may be that an institutional organisation would be able to gain 'official' access to data more easily than individuals.

12 Handling the data

The problems of simplifying raw data and making them appropriate for school use will necessarily remain for teachers. The knowledge explosion implies that the problem will become more acute.

Computers and quantification

As far as storage is concerned we can look forward to the increasing use of the computer and its memory banks. Emphasis at the moment in geography is on using data banks for the storage of objective examination questions, and on developing the computer's handling of processing of locational data. At least three projects are under way which are considering the use and application of the computer in school geography. We can expect them to suggest mathematical and statistical uses. Hand electronic calculators with memories are available to do much of this kind of work. We can expect them to suggest ways in which computers can simulate and test the effect of changing relationships between variables. They may also suggest ways in which computers can be used to construct simple models which can then be tested against real data. They will recommend use of visual display terminals which can handle the patterns of points, lines and areas, in two- and three-dimensional form.

All these are direct and immediate possibilities. The industrial and commercial world makes use of computers in all these ways. Computer use is still on the fringes of much locational study in universities. There are, of course, significant exceptions. Whether computer use becomes routine in universities or schools depends on economic considerations. The telephone link system seems the most likely way ahead in schools, coupled with hand electronic calculator use. Much of the overemphasis and drudgery of mathematical and statistical manipulation which both university student, school teachers and pupils find so wearing should disappear as the century progresses.

Theories and scientific method

The basic model of scientific method as the framework within which location data are handled is likely to remain, but not unchallenged.

Effective computer handling of the data explosion might bring about a revival of the inductive approach, as a more significant route to understanding than of late. This is very difficult to predict. It is easier to predict, however, that normative theory formation will continue to flourish. For computer's can test models quickly and effectively against large quantities of real world data. Much more subjective and socially or politically determined models are likely to become commonly used in universities. They will be used not only for analytic purposes, but in order to attempt to influence perception of location and locational decision making.

This trend is already evident, as readers of *Social Justice and the City* (Harvey 1973) will have observed. In this book Harvey appears to chronicle his own approaches to the study of urban landscapes, and offers at the end of the book a Marxist analysis of the structure of Western capitalist cities, primarily American ones. The thought of presenting overtly a Marxist critique of urban structures in schools may well cause alarm in some quarters. Presented alongside other critiques it should not do so. Some recent books for use in schools, might also cause concern at present in some quarters. In *Where You're At* (Goodey 1974), for instance, the topic headings of the book, which is about place, indicate something of the nature of the way data are being handled. For example, the sequence of headings in chapter 1 runs 'places, labels, ownership, barriers, the bigger the better, and hierarchy'. Chapter 2 starts with the heading 'small places, keep off the grass, who owns you?, the property game, and a question of identity'. The use of normative theory appears to be developing beyond postulating what might be, and is appearing in the presentation of committed viewpoints. These developments in geography are, of course, paralleled by the preparation of similar material for use in school in some other subject areas within the humanities and social sciences.

Publications, if they present one-sided value judgements upon location facts and the reasons for location decision making, raise cause for concern. The presentation of alternative viewpoints, preferably as expounded by their authors, is a different matter. *Utopia* (Ward 1974) overtly looks at alternative views, an approach which most teachers would find acceptable. Indeed, the trend evident in the Geography for the Young School Leaver project of printing newspaper extracts, parts of official documents, and conflicting views on issues in other forms, can only be welcomed.

Abandonment of the rigour and logic which support the structure of scientific method in school geography would be a detrimental step, and teachers may, I fear, have to work hard to maintain a clear distinction between what is and what ought to be, as the century progresses. This does not imply that teachers should see themselves in geography as individuals necessarily concerned to maintain the *status quo*. It does mean that they should maintain high standards of scholarship, and encourage pupils in careful and accurate data collection, statistically sound sampling and the use of appropriate processing devices. In this way, whatever view one may hold of what ought to be can be applied to sound facts. In maintaining this principle, along with the other sciences, geography can make a continuingly useful contribution to education in general. Perception studies, involving the construction of normative theory from mass observation records, are likely to grow. As stated earlier, they, like normative theory, can offer considerable illumination and provide an interesting style of study in schools. Teachers must avoid their becoming deception studies.

The systems model

The switch from the study of unique location in geography to an emphasis on the links which bind features together in the geographical landscape has helped to make pupils aware of the interdependent nature of societies and nations. The systems model, because it can handle three dimensions more easily than two-dimensional spatial models, is likely to become the dominant conceptual model in research, university teaching and schools for a number of years. It is simple in outline, but can handle all levels of complexity. Moreover, as a universal model it matches the spirit of the times in political terms also. There is a growing international awareness that decisions cannot be taken in isolation. Near instant international communication networks and satellite surveillance have shrunk the world to almost village size. In *The Ecology of Natural Resources* (Simmons 1974) a most illuminating geographical view of the application of systems theory to location study can be found. It can provide teachers in school with excellent starter material and hard data presented in systems terms.

But neither the systems model nor computer assisted learning will necessarily solve problems, though they are likely to enable us to handle locational study more effectively. Geographical theories are simply likely to have a higher level of probability and greater powers of illumination than now. Geographers are unlikely to produce immutable location laws — nor, given the human variable, should we expect this to be the case.

13 Environmental impact studies

Where will geography fit into the curriculum of the future? There is already a clear trend to combine geography with other subjects in school. Provided that geographers are absolutely clear as to their contribution to learning, further combining or regrouping of subject matter for school study is not necessarily to be feared.

Problem studies in location

LOCAL SCALE ACTION STUDIES
If geographers handle data, using the systems model and scientific method together, then a much more multidisciplinary approach to study is likely to develop in the universities. Study is also likely to go on to become more problem oriented, and applied geography will grow. Except on a very limited scale, pupils in school cannot expect to solve many problems but they may increasingly have to live with the outcomes of multidisciplinary problem focused research and its impact on everyday life. One can foresee some exercises with real life outcomes, however. A mis-match problem starter, from the Geography 14—18 Project, presented a plan of a house and garden which teacher and pupils could consider, possibly redesigning paths and garden layout. Perhaps some enterprising teacher had already set this problem, using his own garden plan, and then taken the class home at weekends to do the work! Within the school buildings and

playing fields, I am sure other real life locational decision making can take place. One can think of the multidisciplinary nature of the problem of laying out stalls and tents for a school fête, with the knowledge, on the one hand, that it has been laid out for years in the same way by the school's deputy head, and, on the other, that there have been complaints that no one visits the distant stalls. Compound this with heavy overnight rain causing patchy waterlogging, and 3C and their geography teacher, who had been detailed to set up the stalls, would have a problem on their hands.

REGIONAL PREDICTIVE STUDIES

With more regional data available, I could imagine that many problem focused studies would not simply be testing theory against reality, but using theory to predict future outcomes. Limited studies of this kind are not unknown in schools. Studies have been made, for example, to predict likely future land use, based upon field data collection of present land use. On the broad scale, the publication of local authority 'strategy plans' and central government regional studies may have predetermined broad categories of land use. In this case, in school, predictive study would have to work within a finer categorisation than strategic plans usually do. Predicting shopping precinct or petrol station locations in areas designated for housing would be an example.

Predictive studies need not, of course, involve the use of live issues. By using simulation, future location and patterns can be predicted. The theoretical outcome can then be evaluated and modifications made to the simulation, to try to produce something viewed as more desirable or effective. Traffic engineers often work in this way, and pupils could equally well learn to handle traffic flow data and examine outcomes. Very simple computer programs allow the study of queueing problems, for example.

LARGE-SCALE STUDIES

For some time now in the United States, industrial corporations have had to present 'environmental impact' statements to accompany proposals for industrial development. In Australia too they are about to become normal practice. Statements about siting developments in particular places will have to be presented at local scale, stating disturbance or benefit to local inhabitants and indicating physical effects on the landscape and atmosphere. In state terms, cost-benefit analysis will have to be presented, involving social as well as economic costings. In national terms, a third statement indicating likely benefit to the Australian economy as a whole will be necessary. The potential scope for involving geographers will be clear. Data presented in this type of format, showing the interlocking nature of systems, and locational decision making impacts at differing scales, could form remarkably pertinent material for school geographical studies. Such an approach presents a clear model which could be used to revive regional studies. Indeed in these terms, I would expect just such a revival to take place. The first text by a geographer using this approach, at differing regional scales, has still to be written.

Likely trends in topics

STUDY OF THE OCEANS AND SEA BED

The general reader of newspapers and follower of television news and drama serials is aware of the growing economic and political interest in these topics. North Sea oil has in fact hit the classroom in several simulation and study packs, but fishing in geography lessons remains a dated study. Too often, fishing fleets in the United Kingdom are grossly overestimated, and drifters go on catching herring, where neither exist. Apart from oil and fish, the oceans and sea beds are, as yet, relatively ignored. I imagine national territorial claims, if agreed internationally, and the developing technology of sea bed mining, or plankton culture, may encourage much closer study in the next twenty-five years.

LIVING SPACE

It is also possible that combined studies syllabuses will cohere about the problem of living space. What might be called the 'population explosion' is likely to make this true. A doubling of the world's population in the next thirty years can hardly be avoided. So I would expect urban studies to continue to thrive in schools, and economic geography to take on an even more problem oriented approach than it possesses now. The burden of feeding and maintaining the urban societies within which most school children live may not become too pressing in the United Kingdom, but it will in many other parts of the world.

Conclusion

Geography can stand as a subject study timetabled in its own right, if it focuses on location clearly. Within combined studies it should also have an assured place. Themes, problems and approaches to study may change. It is the geography teacher's task to see that curriculum reorganisation does not preclude study of location in schools.

14 Community, home and school

When is geography to be learnt in the future? It is largely an activity labelled in schools and universities, but not widely labelled outside these institutions in everyday life. Departments of geography are unique to learning institutions. Does this mean that learning geography will be confined to the ages of five to twenty-five, if you take a Ph.D., and then largely dispensed with by most people? This question and the question as to whether any significantly new sequencing of geographical learning in schools is likely both deserve consideration here.

Community

Reference was made earlier to the work of Piaget on the child's perception of personal space before the age of five. Reference has also been made to problem oriented research, and the locational decision making which effects everyday life. Location study cannot easily be confined within the bounds of formal education, any more than most studies. The concept of permanent education, elaborated in a number of international reports (Council of Europe 1970), has direct implications for the sequencing of locational study in schools. For, if education is to be viewed as a lifelong process and not a process which becomes increasingly vocationally oriented until it becomes work training, then this perspective opens up a variety of possibilities for sequencing study. The degree to which 'permanent education' will become reality, and the most appropriate pace of development towards such a goal, are clearly matters for debate, as may be also the desirability of such an idea. However, faced with the rapidity of change and the functional redundancy of many jobs which formerly might have been jobs for life, industrial and locational retraining concerned with the acquisition of new skills is growing apace in industrialised societies. The drift from the land is producing similar if unorganised retraining of vast populations throughout the world. To my mind, vocational retraining alone is a dangerously restricted method of coping with change. Education, as opposed to training, is vital as an instrument to cope with change. This means education on a large scale, though recurrently rather than continuously. The most obvious vehicles for this are radio and television. I make the point of the need for mass education, because simply providing for the updating of the skills or knowledge of a minority who have become specialists in an area of study has to me unacceptable political overtones.

Geographers must not be the only people to gain greater understanding of locational variables. Society at large must be offered the opportunity to update its understanding. A growing gap in understanding between locational decision makers and those who have to live with the results could cause increasing social unrest.

This need not happen if teachers became alive to the necessity to press for educational development on a broad front. Geographers have plenty to offer. *World in Action* and *Man Alive* would benefit from the contribution of geographers arguing locational issues. Fewer programmes on television about 'lost worlds' would be a good idea.

Home

Teachers in the classroom now need not wait for major political decision making to implement the setting of geography learning in a wider context. Parental visions of what their children study in geography lessons can be little short of alarming. The primary schools have shown a lead in involving parents in active learning programmes by running classes to explain the 'new' mathematics, for example. Teachers of geography in secondary schools could be doing the same, and I hope they will as time progresses.

School

If lifelong education does develop, and we have the will to see that it does, how will this affect work within the present traditional school years. I could anticipate sequencing from known to unknown, small to large scale, concrete to abstract, and from description towards explanation, to remain the order of the day for the foreseeable future. But it is by no means as clear that work should be set quite so markedly, initially and sometimes dominantly, in local settings. For it is not necessarily the case that what is known must be local. The trend towards more and more local study is not altogether desirable, for pupils' interests based upon non-school activities have brought them into contact with larger-scale environments more often and at an earlier age. Holiday travel at home and abroad, contact with relatives overseas, following the home football team, regular television viewing of *The World About Us*, have all given children a simple knowledge base which is much wider than in the past. Geography teachers can sequence work by starting with any of this already familiar knowledge.

I would expect starters from varied and widely scattered environments to be a growing feature of geographical study, particularly if used as the basis for self-selected topics of work by pupils. Teachers alive to the need to combine curiosity, motivation and effective learning will probably move to individual study programmes for pupils. If pupils suggest the topic or area of interest, then from a conceptual stance teachers can sequence the learning of location terms and ideas as appropriate. Building in assessment procedures much more effectively as intrinsic features of learning sequences is under way and may become the norm.

A personalised, extended spiral mode of geographical study could represent future reality.

15 Geography for the future

Those who are five-year-olds this year may well find themselves the decision makers of the year 2026, just fifty years on. If we look back at change over the last fifty years, ponder its effects and the results of the human desire to control territory and exploit the environment, the desirability of geographical education cannot be in doubt. If we add to this our knowledge of inevitable population growth, and the likely stresses in some parts of the world on living space, on energy and industrial raw materials, as well as on food supply, the enjoyableness of our lives as school children and adults is going to depend on the effectiveness with which skills are acquired, knowledge comprehended and decisions made.

Many of these decisions will have physical impact at landscape scale, and affect pupils' lives directly and immediately. Geography has therefore a part to play in education in intrinsic terms, because it gives pupils command of the language of locational study. More than ever, it will also need to be seen to contribute to debates about the nature of society as a whole.

Geographers had a part to play in the explorers' world of the past, they are playing a part in the exploited world of the present, and they must play a part in the educated world of the future.

References *and* Name index

ABLER, P., ADAMS, J. S. and GOULD, P. (1970) *Spatial Organisation: A Geographer's View of the World.* New York, Prentice Hall. *1, 10, 93*

BALCHIN, W. G. V. (1972) Graphicacy. *Geography,* **57,** 185–95. *24*

BENNETTS, T. (1973) The nature of geographical objectives. In R. Walford (ed.), *New Directions in Geography Teaching,* 160–72. London, Longman. *56*

BLOOM, B. S. (1956) (ed.) *Taxonomy of Educational Objectives, Handbook I: Cognitive Domain.* London, Longman. *22*

BLYTH, W. A. L. and others (1976) *Curriculum Planning in History, Geography and Social Science.* London, Collins/E.S.L. *61*

BRUNER, J. S. (1962) *The Process of Education.* Cambridge, Massachusetts, Harvard University Press. *47, 59*

CARSON, S. McB. (1971) (ed.) *Environmental Studies: The Construction of an A Level Syllabus.* London, National Foundation for Educational Research. *42*

CHAPALLAZ, D. P., DAVIS, P. F., FITZGERALD, B. P. and others (1970) Hypothesis testing in field studies. *Teaching Geography,* **2.** Sheffield, Geographical Association. *84*

COLE, J. P. and BEYNON, N. J. (1968) *New Ways in Geography.* Books 1 and 2. Oxford, Basil Blackwell. *8*

COUNCIL OF EUROPE (1970) *Permanent Education.* Strasbourg, Council of Europe. *119*

CRAWFORD, S. (1970–2) *Man Alone. Living Together. A New Man. Man Organises.* In The Developing World series, ed. R. Pitcher. London, Longman. *44*

CROMARTY, D. (1975) Reconstructing the syllabus. *Teaching Geography,* **1,** 28–31. London, Longman/Geographical Association. *10*

DAVIES, W. K. D. (1972) (ed.) *Conceptual Revolution in Geography.* London, University of London Press. *4*

DAVIS, W. M. (1954) *Geographical Essays.* New York, Dover. *13*

DEPARTMENT OF EDUCATION AND SCIENCE (1967) *Children and Their Primary Schools.* London, H.M.S.O. *56*

DEPARTMENT OF EDUCATION AND SCIENCE (1972) *New Thinking in School Geography.* London, H.M.S.O. *56*

DEPARTMENT OF EDUCATION AND SCIENCE (1974) *School Geography in the Changing Curriculum.* Education Survey No 19. London, H.M.S.O. *2, 11, 16, 37, 41, 42, 43*

ELLIOTT, G. (1975) *Putting 'Place' on the Map.* Occasional Paper No 4, Schools Council History, Geography and Social Science 8–13 project. Liverpool, School of Education. *60*

ELLIOTT, G. (1976) *Teaching for Concepts.* London, Collins/E.S.L. *65*

GAGNÉ, R. M. (1965) *The Conditions of Learning.* New York, Holt, Rinehart and Winston. *55*

GELSTHORPE, A. P. and HALSALL, D. A. (1975) Sixth form fieldwork in urban geography. *The Classroom Geographer,* April 1975, 2–17. Luton, Sealey. *84*

GOODEY, B. (1974) *Where You're At.* London, Penguin Education. *112*

GOULD, P. and WHITE, R. (1974) *Mental Maps.* Harmondsworth, Penguin. *11*

HAGGETT, P. (1972) *Geography: A Modern Synthesis.* London and New York, Harper and Row. *10, 93*

HARVEY, D. (1973) *Social Justice and the City.* London, Arnold. *112*

HICKMAN, G., REYNOLDS, J. and TOLLEY, H. (1973) *A New Professionalism for a Changing Geography.* London, Schools Council. *81*

JOINT MATRICULATION BOARD (1974) *Geography (Advanced) Syllabus B: Notes for the guidance of teachers on the internal assessment of competence in practical skills and techniques. 94, 98*

JOINT MATRICULATION BOARD (1975) *General Certificate of Education Regulations and Syllabuses: 1977. 92*

KRATHWOHL, D. R. and others (1964) *Taxomony of Educational Objectives, Handbook II: Affective Domain.* London, Longman. *22, 23*

OXFORD GEOGRAPHY PROJECT (1974, 1975) Preface to Books 1, 2 and 3. London, Oxford University Press. *10*

PETERS, R. S. (1963) *Education as Initiation.* London, Evans. *54*

PIAGET, J. and INHELDER, B. (1956) *The Child's Conception of Space.* London, Routledge and Kegan Paul. *23*

REYNOLDS, J. and STEVENS, G. T. (1974) Geography 14–18 O level paper. *Bulletin of Environmental Education,* October 1974. *81*

RUSHBY, J. G., BELL, J. and DYBECK, M. W. (1971) *Study Geography Stage Five.* London, Longman. *18*

SAUVY, J. and SAUVY, S. (1974) *The Child's Discovery of Space.* London, Penguin Education. *23*

SCHOOLS COUNCIL (1970) The environmental studies approach. *Dialogue,* **6**, 7–9. *42*

SCHOOLS COUNCIL (1971) *Social Studies 8–13.* Working Paper 39. London. *39*

References and Name index

SCHOOLS COUNCIL (1974, 1975) *Man, Land and Leisure. People, Place and Work. Cities and People.* Geography for the Young School Leaver project. London, Nelson. *15*

SCHOOLS COUNCIL (1975) *Curriculum Research and Development in Environmental Education.* London. *41*

SIMMONS, I. G. (1974) *The Ecology of Natural Resources.* London, Arnold. *114*

SKINNER, B. F. (1953) *Science and Human Behavior.* New York, Collier-Macmillan. *47*

SMITH, T. J. (1975) (ed.) *The Politics of Physical Resources.* London, Penguin Education/Open University Press. *89*

STOPP, P. (1973) Bibliography of games and simulations. *The Classroom Geographer*, May, November, December 1973. Luton, Sealey. *32*

TAYLOR, P. (1970) *How Teachers Plan Their Courses.* London, National Foundation for Educational Research. *54, 55*

WALFORD, R. (1969) *Games in Geography.* London, Longman. *32*

WARD, C. (1974) *Utopia.* London, Penguin Education. *113*

WARD, C. and FYSON, A. (1973) *Streetwork: The Exploding School.* London, Routledge and Kegan Paul. *45*

Subject index

aims, 55–8
assessment, 29, 79, 81–4, 89, 95–8, 105–6
 data response questions, 96–7
 essay questions, 96
 internal assessment, 95, 98
 objective teaching, 97–8
 practical individual projects, 82, 84–5, 94–5
attitude development, 32–6

case studies, 18, 94
Certificate in Secondary Education, 79, 86
combined studies, 38–44
common core examinations, 81–2
community, 119
computers, 108–9, 111
concentric studies, 15–16
concepts, 6–11, 62–9, 93, 100–2, 106
conceptual studies, 15–16
Crewe Girls Grammar School, 60–1
curriculum change, 54–69, 70–9, 80–90

earth sciences, 45
environmental studies, 41–2, 115–18

Fearnhill School, Letchworth, 80–90
field studies, 21, 25, 81, 84

General Certificate in Education
 A Level, 91–9
 O Level, 80–90
geography
 applied, 15, 115–17
 human, 93–4
 junior school, 37–8
 physical, 92–3
 secondary school, 37–45

hand-eye coordination, 24–5
home, 120
humanities, 41

integrated studies, 40–3
interdisciplinary studies, 43–4

Joint Matriculation Board, 91–9

knowledge
 analysis, 29–30
 application, 28–9
 comprehension, 27–8, 96–7
 evaluation, 31–2
 explosion, 107–10
 learning, 25–32
 synthesis, 30

living space, 117–18

Subject index

local studies, 42–3, 115–16

maps, use of, 17, 24, 28, 48–50
models, 8–11, 93
   equilibrium, 13
   gravity, 47
   systems, 11, 13, 50–1, 114

Northicote High School, Wolverhampton, 100–6

objectives, 59–60, 70–1, 100
   examinations, 94, 96–9
oceans, 117

perception studies, 11, 113
permanent education, 119–21
photographs, use of, 17, 25, 108
predictive study, 116
project dissemination, 77–8, 84, 86, 89

quantitative techniques, 5, 29

regional studies, 16–20, 50–1, 116–17
resources, 76–7, 100–1

Schools Council
   Geography 14–18 Project, 33–4, 80–90
   Geography for the Young School Leaver Project, 14–15, 70–9
   History, Geography and Social Science 8–13, Project, 56–9
scientific method, 4–6
simulation, 31–2
skills, 22–5, 94–5
social studies, 40–1
stream tables, 48–9
systematic studies, 11–16, 48–50

television, 100, 105, 121
thematic studies, 14–15
theories, 8–11, 112–13

urban studies, 44–5, 100–6
University of Cambridge Local Examination Syndicate, 81

visual observation, 22–4, 25

Westwood High School, Leek, 71
worksheets, 100, 102
world studies, 43